The Healing Sorrow WORKBOOK

Rituals for Transforming Grief and Loss

Peg Elliott Mayo, L.C.S.W.

Foreword by David Feinstein, Ph.D.

New Harbinger Publications, Inc.

Distributed in the U.S.A. by Publishers Group West; in Canada by Raincoast Books; in Great Britain by Airlift Book Company, Ltd.; in South Africa by Real Books, Ltd.; in Australia by Boobook; and in New Zealand by Tandem Press.

Copyright © 2001 by Peg Elliott Mayo
        New Harbinger Publications, Inc.
        5674 Shattuck Avenue
        Oakland, CA 94609

Cover design by Lightbourne Images
Edited by Carole Honeychurch
Text design by Michele Waters

ISBN 1-57224-240-X Paperback

New Harbinger Publications' Web site address: www.newharbinger.com

03   02   01

10   9   8   7   6   5   4   3   2   1

First printing

This book is for
Patrick—he'd be so amazed!
Katie, Stan, and Peter—they lived it, too.
David—he expected it.
Don—he supported it.

Contents

Gratitudes

As I think back over all the years this book has been a-borning, a parade of faces passes my mind's eye. There are clients, who with their suffering and struggles, inspired new approaches and strong feelings. We entered the fire together and emerged refined. There was my father, whose life was an example and testament to the healing qualities of taking the long, karmic view of existence. And my first husband, Joe Pleskunas, and son, Patrick, who, four years apart, chose death over life. In so doing, they confronted me and the rest of the family with horror, sorrow, and, ultimately, compassion. It was this passage—this *process*—that has provided much of the grist for this book. To Joe and Patrick I offer a strange and sincere "thank you," for your choices have forced much spiritual awakening. Others—too many to list—have taught by example what a privileged treasure it is to live on this glorious planet.

Don Pauls, my life partner, has patiently and persistently supported my work. He is a quiet man and a deep man. I am profoundly grateful to have had these years with him.

David Feinstein, exemplar of friendship, boon companion, powerful mentor, and all around good sport rates sixty pages (at least) of appreciations, but this is all he gets—this book.

Etta Linton, Dan Long, and April Fisher all cast their eagle's eye on the manuscript and found it rich in peculiar typos, creative spelling, ruptured syntax, and challengeable assumptions. These whimsies they have done their best to point out. What has been done since, of course, is nobody's responsibility except my own.

Patrick Fanning, one of the founders of New Harbinger Publications, has been not only kind and efficient but quick in his responses—sterling qualities. Carole Honeychurch, my editor, has understood from the start what this book is about, something I much appreciate.

Thank you all. I am most grateful.

Peg Elliott Mayo
The Land, Coast Range of Oregon
September 15, 2000

Foreword

David Feinstein, Ph.D.

You are holding in your hands uncommon instruction about how to live. It is written by one of the most effective psychotherapists on the planet, who, upon having crossed the threshold of her seventy-first year, is determined to leave in her books the hard-earned wisdom of a remarkable life well-lived. Through the multiplier effect of the printed page, the opportunity is yours to apprentice yourself here and now to an extraordinary mentor, learning how to transform life's inevitable losses into wisdom and competence.

If this is a guide about how to live better, why begin with grief and loss? Because it is from our encounters with despair that we are most ready to engage ourselves in the good work of healing the wounds and changing the mental habits that limit our joy, effectiveness, and fulfillment. If you look carefully, you can only conclude that our capacity for delight is far higher on the evolutionary scale than our inclination to avoid pain. Pleasure is, in fact, our most wholesome and exquisite drive. For proof, simply watch an infant. This is a pleasure-motivated being, capable of fresh gratification from every form of agreeable sensory stimulation. We humans have evolved with a greater concentration of endorphin receptors, the chemical basis for the experience of pleasure, than any other creature, and these receptors are ingeniously paired with our capacities to love and to learn. As neurochemist Candace Pert summarizes it, "We are wired for pleasure!"

Threats to our survival, however, take precedence over pleasure. The fight-flight-or-freeze response, controlled by the sympathetic nervous system, is not concerned about your enjoyment of the process—only that you survive it. The loss of a loved one is a psychological amputation, a shock for which we can never be fully prepared, as are losses of health, function, and even dreams. Each loss takes us on an uninvited journey into dark hollows of the human soul. We may return wiser and ready to reengage. We may return blinded by the light, closed to pleasure, retreading the pain endlessly until our sensibilities are dulled. The emotional wounds of our childhoods, and the patterns they set into motion also alienate us from the pleasure-based guidance system that is a pinnacle of evolution. And because the stresses of modern life are unrelenting, they too erode our capacity to experience and learn from pleasure.

This book is a guide for renewing your relationship with pleasure—not a frivolous objective. It promises nothing less than to reestablish for you a more wholesome guidance system as you move forward in a culture that places on your path an unprecedented cascade of mean-spirited obstacles while daring you to enjoy the journey.

More than a set of ideas and attitudes, *The Healing Sorrow Workbook* is a step-by-step program for healing both recent and antiquated wounds, transforming outmoded habits of thought and action, and embodying a more wholesome philosophy of life and loss. Woven throughout the text, with its abiding humor and good spirit, are fifty personal rituals. Active by nature, they are brilliantly designed to garner the lessons of your history, your senses, and your ability to reflect, and to embed these lessons deeply into your body, mind, and spirit.

The sequence of topics is itself instructive. In briefest summary, the book begins by addressing the nature of consciousness, the dynamics of sorrow, and the place of hope. It proceeds to show you how to repair inner schisms, envision a new tomorrow, express what is in the depths of your soul, and leave behind what can no longer be. It closes by guiding you to become a midwife in the rebirth of your own capacity for pleasure. However this book came into your hands, regardless of your level of hope or despair, I invite you to engage yourself fully in what could be a remarkable journey that sets a new tone for your future.

INTRODUCTION

Shades of Sorrow

When you've drunk the bitter cupful, you will find a rare jewel in the bottom.

—B. A. Elliott

Sorrow is no stranger to anyone's life, and is usually associated with loss, grief, and uninvited change. It may be tied to a loss of status or role, as when a marriage ends or the last child leaves home. Some suffer at the loss of place: a desert lover who is required to live in a Northeastern city. Who has not felt emotional pain at the fading of a friendship? We anguish over lost illusions and unrealized hopes.

Grief, which is the most profound form of sorrow, is a natural, predictable response to bereavement, as when a loved one dies or when catastrophic illness is diagnosed. Depression and even despair—which is the absence of hope—frequently result, sometimes with lifelong effect. And yet, most people outlive the events that elicit sadness, some with enviable enrichment of deeper understanding and improved function. This does not happen by accident—there are specific principles involved.

From Life's Wounds to the Rebirth of Pleasure

Pleasure is a deceptively simple thing. It is the capacity to enjoy, appreciate, savor, and participate painlessly with life. As grief is the most profound of sorrows, so bliss is the acme of pleasures. There are an infinitely varied array of intensities, depending on the individual personality and circumstances. I choose to focus on *pleasure* rather than bliss, ecstasy, creativity, or even happiness, because all of these are implied possibilities flowing from the ability to respond with pleasure. We all long to feel satisfaction, comfort, engagement, and power—these feelings reflect mobilized energy and give much of life its meaning.

When the events of life leave us feeling wounded, inadequate, helpless, or hopeless, then pleasure is fugitive and purpose is lost. The rebirth of pleasure—a smile, savoring a meal, responding to some cleverness or amusing activity—is a clear sign that balance is returning.

For almost forty years as a clinical social worker in both public institutions and private practice, I have been the privileged witness of the lives of others in intimate moments of suffering and revitalization. One truth stands out clearly against the background of suffering: the human spirit is astoundingly and blessedly resilient. Certainly there are those who lack the stamina or wherewithal to summon their forces and transform their misery into a deeper understanding of life's processes. We can only mourn for them, for it is not given to anyone to make the decision to affirm life for another. We must each do so for ourselves.

This affirmation is the undeniable result of free will, which says that, ultimately, it is our own *choices* of attitude and behavior that shape our response to the challenges of life. Let's imagine that five people eat an identical meal in a restaurant and all become sick. There will be five different responses, each dependent on the attitude and behavior of the individual. The first will bitterly decide to sue. The second will discern a conspiracy by agribusiness to degrade the food supply. The third will decide it is divine retribution for going off a proscribed diet. The fourth may decide it's too dangerous to ever to eat a meal out again and the fifth will say, "That's the breaks—this time the odds caught up with me."

This is not to say that we cannot or should not effectively and generously offer our skills, support, blessings, and energies to others, but it is up to them to use what is offered. I have often felt sorrow at this necessary codicil on free will.

I have witnessed and, hopefully, sometimes catalyzed many stunning recoveries from daunting challenges. The courageous recoveries I've seen are what give me hope. I trust you will find them both inspiring and instructive as you work through your own grief process. Throughout this book you will be shown true-life examples of triumphs of spirit. For there to be a triumph, there must be a challenge. The story of one of the families I saw in my practice, a family I'll call the Bennetts, will be one theme. My recovery from my husband's and son's suicides is another. There are others. I choose them over a thousand other possibilities because of the complexity of responses involved and the final success gained in transforming a terrible situation with potentially dangerous ramifications into an odyssey of spirit from which all emerged enriched. They are dramatic stories, but the principles are applicable to other situations.

A client I will call Dan Bennett, a child psychologist, was forty-one when he was diagnosed with liver cancer. Despite the pleadings and raging of his wife, Sylvia, he refused the most common medical interventions of chemotherapy and radiation. The couple had two children, Michael, twelve, and Teddy, only three. Their crisis came in midst of a delightful life involving sailing, crafts, writing, financial stability, professional success, and a solid marriage. All were cast into dark perspective with the diagnosis.

It has long been my practice to tape record or keep a personal journal following the progress of my clients. The following is an excerpt from Dan's initial disclosure as recorded in my journal.

> *He didn't take long. I don't think I'll ever forget his words: "Doctor MacAlbee has just told me I should plan on winding things up in the next four months—it seems I've got the 'Big C.'" His voice was flat as Kansas, and only the strange glitter in his eyes showed any emotion.*
>
> *I told him of my disbelief, all the while searching his face and body for clues. I had noticed he was losing weight, but anyone who works and plays as hard as Dan, is likely to get a little gaunt once in a while. Now I could see he looked sallow, holding his mouth stiffly, as if he didn't trust his self-control. It took me a minute to realize how awful it must be for him to have to persuade me he was dying.*
>
> *He filled in the details of weird symptoms, Silvia's insistence on the medical workup, and what it might mean financially and practically for his family. It was as if*

he had totally mobilized his intellect for dealing with the crisis—as if all his emotions, intuition and spontaneity were turned off, too. We sat there talking like mechanical people.

Then he came up with his mind-boggling idea. I want to record what he said as accurately as I can remember: "Look, Peg, I've been a therapist for seventeen years. I know what this kind of thing does to a family. It brings out the weaknesses. It sometimes breaks people—not that I think that'll happen here, but who knows? Anyhow, Teddy is just a baby and Mike is at a pretty critical stage of his development. I don't want to mess up these last few months I've got left. Sylvia will take it hard, but will stiff-upper-lip it. What I want you to do is hang around, be our friend and therapist."

Dan had applied his best judgment and asked for help in his crisis. Typically, he thought of those dearest to him before himself. Some of this was, of course, a defense against the horror of his personal situation. Some things are very hard to bear and an inner wisdom allows us to come gradually into realization. John O'Donahue, a compassionate priest who wrote and recorded *Anam Cara* ("Soul Friend" 1996) in Gaelic, speaks of how the soul naturally eases into realization, quite unlike the "neon glare" demanded by modern psychology.

This was not denial. Dan knew he had liver cancer. He knew quite well what his few options were and had an intellectual understanding of the all-but-certain outcome. What he was buffering himself against in making his arrangements was the emotional impact. That, we both knew, would come soon enough.

Sorrow and Pleasure in My Life

As I write, I am seventy-one years old. I am not a mild person and I have lived my life. By that I mean life has not "happened" to me, but I have engaged and wrestled—often impotently and foolishly—with the array of events that have filled my days. I was blessed with ardor for creative expression, a family that nurtured it, a profession that supports it, and a multitude of engrossing avocations. I have felt and received much love. And I have lived through the horrors and wonders of much of the twentieth century.

There have been life-altering losses: my mother's death from asthma when I was twelve, my husband's and son's suicides, my father's passing when he was only a year older than I am now. I have lost status and role, place and vision, physical capacity and illusion, people I loved and animals that filled my heart with joy. But I have never lost hope.

"Hope of *what?*" is a fair question. Hope of learning and creating as well as hope of clearing my karma through right action. In my often halting, derailed, and clumsy movement toward individuation, I have required much help. The help has come by way of interventions by friends, sudden illuminations, and a lot personal pick-and-shovel emotional-spiritual work. And it has taken time alone in nature to find perspective on my processes.

The Eastern European poet, Vaclav Havel, wrote clearly on the nature of hope.

Either we have hope within us or we don't;
It is a dimension of the soul, and it's not essentially
Dependent on some particular observation of the World
Or estimate of the situation. Hope is not prognostication.
It is an orientation of the spirit, an orientation of the heart;

It transcends the world that is immediately experienced,
and is anchored somewhere beyond its horizons. . . .

Hope, in this deep and powerful sense, is not the same as joy
that things are going well, or willingness to invest in enterprises
that are obviously headed for success, but, rather, an ability
to work for something because it is good, not just because it stands
a chance to succeed. The more propitious the situation in which
we demonstrate hope, the deeper the hope is. Hope is
definitely not the same thing as optimism.
It is not the conviction that something will turn
out well, but the certainty that something
makes sense, regardless of how it turns out.

Pleasure now comes easily to me. I savor a good book, the touch of a hand, creative time and a host things both more dramatic and even simpler. It's a bit of a brag, but the truth is I have a gift for happiness, appreciation, and spontaneous fun. This has not always been so, and I suppose I will again experience my range to feel sorrow, confusion, and anger. This balanced potential is part of my—and your—human condition as we engage with life.

A conscious person is aware of choices. This is both blessing and burden and in both cases it is clear that we are responsible for what we do, don't do, or passively allow to happen. How often I have wished that someone, somehow, would make a decision for me. Will I live or die? Will I take revenge, become embittered, or somehow transcend the present suffering? Possibilities abound and with them often comes confusion. It is the agency of free will—personal responsibility to choose a path—that defines our lives. Even procrastination or indecision is a choice to drift and stay in the suffering. Sometimes the burden of choice requires growth that we had no idea we were capable of making.

Karma and Individuation

In the previous paragraphs, I used the terms "karma" and "individuation." Defining these ideas is important, for they provide the context for this entire book on transcending sorrow. My father explained *karma* very simply. "Life," he said, "is a day in school. Study hard so you'll be promoted next time around, not held back or demoted." Implied in that are the ideas that the present moment—present life—precious as it is, is not all there is to existence, that our task is to study and act upon the events life presents in an ethical way, and that there are consequences to our choices.

The same idea is found in the biblical idea that one sows what they reap. Another way of looking at the same idea is condensed in the phrase, "What goes around, comes around." These concepts are roots of the Tree of Knowledge: they offer incentive to growth and fulfillment. Nowhere is it written that such maturation is simple or easy.

Individuation is the drive innate in humankind to fill in our gaps, accumulate and digest many experiences (which is called wisdom), and to become all that our nature allows. It suggests that we come equipped to change, grow, refine, and thrive in a world of challenges. Those who stop stretching, exploring, risking, and consciously choosing—the poor souls who are frozen in some prison of thought and expectations—suffocate the urgent need to individuate. Once again, individuation is the gift we give ourselves by being willing to integrate learning with experience and reflect it in our life choices. It is the Everest of life.

What This Book Is About and How to Use It

This is a book about the common themes of sorrow and how they may be wholesomely addressed. The purpose and goal is the rebirth of pleasure. It includes many exercises or "rituals" to gently challenge and guide you from the "dark night of the soul" to an enriched, wiser, more compassionate consciousness in which pleasure is integrated. It is about using the resources within you to transform the aching void of loss into the vitality of pleasurable engagement. While reading, you will find many examples of how others have made the passage from profound unhappiness to living creatively. This is do-able work, if you are diligent in guarding your flicker of hope and following through the natural steps of transformation. That you are reading right now demonstrates hope. I suggest you read the book all the way through before doing the rituals and then work through them systematically, for that is how you will realize the greatest benefit.

The first part of the book, "The Pairing of Despair and Hope," brings into focus the dual nature of human perception and introduces the principles of alchemical change. Part II, "The Nature and Source of Suffering," discusses some of the sources of sorrow that are found in our separation from ourselves, others, the familiar, positive anticipation, illusions, and a spiritual context. The third part, "Tools for Alchemical Transformation," is the longest section of this book, because once you have learned the means to choose a more vibrant life, you will discover your own marvelous capacity for growth and positive change. Part IV, "Confirming Your Positive Changes," provides ways of bolstering your determination to live well, despite the sorrows that enter every life.

The Rituals

I've chosen the term "rituals" for the activities you'll find distributed throughout this workbook because I like the specialness of the term more than the mundane "exercises." Rituals are acts performed with seriousness (not to be confused with somberness) and dedication. They are part of the process of giving yourself respectful attention and a hopeful focus. I advise having a special place with beautiful things to go to as you concentrate on transforming the sorrows of life to a creative engagement.

You will do well to dedicate an hour several times a week to this life-enhancing process. Retreat to a space where you will not be interrupted. Of course, this is an adaptation of your usual routine, which is what ritual calls for—a time apart from the ordinary demands of modern life. You are engaged in reordering your perspective from bleak sorrow to fertile possibility. Such a mission is worthy of considerable effort.

Your work is personal, intimate, and private. Be cautious about sharing it with others, for then you can avoid self-conscious censoring or posing for even a sympathetic audience. If you do open your work to another, choose the person carefully. Sometimes working with a therapist or trusted friend will support you in difficult moments or offer clarity when you are baffled. I'm simply advising you to be thoughtful and avoid distorting your deepest experiences with concerns about the scrutiny and judgment of others.

Again, I urge you to work sequentially with this material: the rituals are planned for their cumulative effect. Some will take more courage than you knew you had, but the work is a way to satisfaction. Some may seem irrelevant, but probably are not. You will not be graded, there is nothing to be concerned about as far as the mechanics of composition, and the satisfaction of transformative growth will be your reward.

The Challenge

Any change of habits is typically resisted, especially habitual ways of thinking. On one level, you certainly *do* want to address your sorrow and revive pleasure, no question about it. On another level, you have learned how to survive with it and change calls not only for effort, but also for entering a new psychic country. This can be scary, particularly because examining the roots of sorrow means revisiting the events and habits that have entrenched it in your life.

One useful way to meet this challenge is to recognize that you control the pace of change. You may be a person who is deliberate and thorough, taking a measured amount of time to accomplish difficult tasks. You may be a person who is quick and spontaneous in tackling fresh ideas. Neither style is better than the other, they are simply different. We will be looking at your way of "doing business" in ritual 2.

Another important consideration is your overall vision for yourself. Too often we act in our pain like animals in a trap. The misery disorganizes our thoughts and behavior—all we want to do is escape. While this is understandable, it is also incomplete, because once free of the trap, then what? Ritual 3 will help you begin to envision a new way of being, a reward for transforming your anguish into free energy to allocate as you choose.

It could be worthwhile for you to do this work while engaged in counseling or therapy with a practitioner who is familiar with the process. If you find yourself immobilized or frightened by the power of your feelings, do consider seeking out such a trusted person to support your work.

PART I

The Pairing of Despair and Hope

CHAPTER 1

The Paired Inevitabilities: Despair and Hope

There is no good in arguing with the inevitable.
The only argument available with an east wind is to put on your overcoat.

—James Russell Lowell

Human consciousness is designed to see things in opposites—dualities. Up-down, man-woman, good-bad, mind-body, you-me, either-or, sorrow-satisfaction, ecstasy-anguish. Why this is so is the stuff for philosophers and religious mystics, who generally believe this trait is where we spiritually begin our inward journey and, with dedication, where we may hope to have a glimpse of the unity of creation. "All is one" proceeding from some transcendent source beyond our comprehension.

The familiar symbol of the yin-yang makes this complex idea plain.

First there is the circle, a symbol of wholeness, completion, eternity. The circle is gracefully divided into a dark and a light side, suggesting that these qualities fit together intimately. Either hemisphere would be a meaningless abstract shape without its twin. Within the dark is a seed of light, within the light is the seed of darkness. There is beauty in this simple schematic.

We may name each half whatever we will, if we also name its opposite by a contrasting value. In this book, we will consider that sorrow is the dark half and that it carries in its womb the potential for hope. The light half carries deep within the potential for despair. We know that when we love, we are committing ourselves to the potential for loss. There seems no way around it, other than living numb, mechanical lives, which would be wasteful of our creative gifts.

There is a relationship between sorrow and pleasure. We have all known people who have mild temperaments and those who are intense. We have also known those who seem flat or blunted emotionally. We vary infinitely in our energy potentials. The principal to which we will return in this book is that, to whatever degree we are individually capable of experiencing suffering, we also have the potential for that intensity of pleasure. There is hope here!

The Ecstasy-Anguish Scale

In the following diagram, put an "X" where you place yourself at this moment on the ecstasy-anguish continuum. "5" is the extreme; "1" the least magnitude. If you are a "3" on Anguish, rest assured you have the potential to experience a 3 on the upside. Put an exclamation mark there. Sometimes such a graphic itself brings a flutter of excitement—check yourself for it.

Keep in mind that the gray area represents that featureless landscape where feelings are so muted that they're barely recognizable. That area is sometimes engrained through long practice, but it's not a pleasant place to live. At the top of the gray band is maybe a wan smile and, at the bottom, a bland, disengaged acceptance of things as they are. This may feel safe, but it denies the person living there pleasure, satisfaction, belly laughs, and intimacy, which all come only with the investment of energy in their manifestation.

Do not make the mistake of thinking that there is some symmetry here that makes inevitable that for every up, there is a down. That's just not so. We are talking about potential here, nothing more.

The Ecstasy-Anguish Scale

ECSTASY

1

2

3   *!*

4

5

5

4

3   *X*

2

1

ANGUISH

Understanding your range—your highs and lows—gives you power to direct your energy consciously for your own benefit. Once you know where you are in terms of capacity for unhappiness, you also have the information of your potential for pleasure. Take hope and let us move ahead on the healing.

Earlier, I explained that the reason the activities of this book are called "rituals" rather than "exercises" is that the work implies something deeper, something with powerful and serious intentions. Now that you have awareness of your "agony-ecstaty" potential, of the inevitably dual nature of human consciousness, and the necessity to make choices in life, it is time to commit to the work of change.

Ritual 1 is the foundation practice I hope you will integrate into your life. It connects mind, body, and emotions and springs from ancient meditation practices. It is to be performed before every other ritual in this book. In all, you will find fifty opportunities as you work your way forward to perform a ritual designed to further your well-being. Every one of them should begin with ritual 1. It won't take much time, but will provide the vital connections between all parts of your being.

Ritual One: Holistic Breath

I begin each day with this ritual and practice it frequently during the day. It is a refreshment for me and provides a sort of "coming home to myself" that confirms that I am a feeling, thinking, active being. The day I am writing this for you, I awakened to rain sounds and muted light (I live in Oregon). Bed was warm, but the day was calling for engagement, including this writing. Still snuggled in, I fixed my eyes on the form of the big-leaf maple across the creek. I emptied my body of stale air, and with it, the pressure to perform. Then I rested an instant, free of pressure. Then I inhaled fresh air, and with *it*, glad anticipation. Then I was full and energized. That is the whole ritual, something I repeated six or eight times before arising this morning. Now it's your turn.

Gather this book, extra paper or a journal, pen, and good light. Retreat to a quiet place and take the steps necessary to secure your privacy for at least a half hour. This will, in time, become sacred space and dedicated time. Recognize the importance of your intention. Make yourself physically comfortable.You are going to learn "four-stroke breathing" in a moment. The point of it is to center and calm yourself as well as to provide energy and focus. It feels good, too! Four-stroke breathing begins with exhalation, which is cleansing, followed by the second stroke of being empty. The third stroke is filling or refreshing, and the fourth is being full. Let's begin. For the first stroke, you will want to decided which feeling or idea you need to cleanse from your heart and spirit. From the following list, choose one of the most difficult feelings for you at the present moment. If what you know you need to cleanse isn't on the list, add it at the end, in the place provided.

____ fear

____ fatigue

____ confusion

____ helplessness

____ guilt

____ shame

_____ anger

_____ sadness

_____ despair

_____ hate

_____ distrust

_____ cynicism

_____ isolation

_____ _____

Now it's time to choose what emotions or qualities you want to replace the stagnant or hurtful stuff just released with. Again, choose one of the most important at this time for your refreshment. If the quality you most want isn't listed, then add your own at the end.

_____ trust

_____ vitality

_____ clarity

_____ power

_____ satisfaction

_____ worthiness

_____ serenity

_____ pleasure

_____ hope

_____ love

_____ curiosity

_____ connection

_____ _____

Good! Now you have chosen a path of cleansing and refreshment. In each cycle, you will be free to either continue using this pair of emotions or choose another set. Just be sure you choose consciously, selecting what you know you need.

Breathing is the most fundamental of our body's processes. Mystics also hold that it connects us with the rest of creation. When you take conscious charge of your breath, you control not only your physical enrichment, but, by extension, your emotional metabolism.

1. Rest on your back or sit up comfortably. Check yourself for rigidity and do what you can to release it.

2. Lift your chin a little and unlock your jaw to provide an open airway.

3. Rest your ever-searching eyes by closing them or looking softly at a beautiful object.

4. Stroke one: Cleansing. Empty your breath through your mouth as completely as possible using belly muscles and ribs. This takes effort, because the pressure of the air outside the body is greater than that within. So, the metaphor supports the idea that it takes a little extra energy to cleanse used-up or toxic stuff. As you exhale old air, also consciously exhale one of the negative emotions you chose a moment ago. Empty as completely as you can.

5. Stroke two: Being empty. Be empty a moment. Reflect on the reality that you have released unwanted energy.

6. Stroke three: Refreshing. Through your nose (if possible) slooooowly fill up, not only with oxygen for your body's pleasure, but also with one of the positive emotions you've chosen.

7. Stroke four: Being full. Savor the moment of being full of the feeling you've chosen as most desirable.

   You've done it! You've learned four-stroke breathing. It is a wonderful remedy for almost any difficult situation or feeling, easy to do and unobtrusive to perform even in a tense public situation.

8. Now repeat the cycle at least six times. If you lose your focus, just return to the beginning and start over—you'll soon get the hang of it. Do not force an artificial tempo on yourself: breathe in the four-stroke pattern at a pace natural to you. It is unlikely, but if you get dizzy, just stop, move around, get a drink of water, and settle yourself. No harm done! *Always begin your work with ritual one: it prepares your body and spirit for healing.*

It is no secret that we are each unique. There really is no "one size fits all." The greater our depth of self-understanding, the more effectively we can direct our power. When we are self-aware, we are far less likely to be unreasonably demanding on ourselves or fearfully comparing our results with another's. One of the many dimensions of personality is our way of viewing issues and fashioning problem-solving strategies.

Now that you've gained an understanding of your natural way of working, you will find, in the next ritual, a way to create achievable goals and realistic expectations for yourself. In this work, you are gathering practical, applicable information in a systematic way designed to strengthen your resolve and increase your probability of success. Throughout this book, you will discover new facets of your wonderful complexity. Let the self-knowledge accumulate until you know yourself with beautiful, diamond clarity.

Ritual Two: Your Temperament

Julian is a man most comfortable when he has a great deal of information and, as he says, "all the ducks in a row." He is deliberate, systematic, and detail minded. He is "goal oriented," meaning he has an objective clearly in mind. Martin is quite different. He loves to "just run with" ideas and impulses. He is inclined to experiment and learn from the process, the goal being important but secondary. Both are effective; they are simply different. It is useful to recognize and honor the ways you learn and change most naturally.

Choose the characteristics most honestly descriptive of your temperament.

____ 1. I care a lot about details in my work.

____ 2. I am most interested in the overall ideas, rather than details.

____ 3. I am a careful person in most regards.

____ 4. I am inclined to take risks or experiment.

____ 5. I like to "get a picture" of the objective when I begin to work or learn.

____ 6. It is my way to gather an impression and go by feelings or instinct.

____ 7. I am usually aware of time passing.

____ 8. I characteristically lose track of time.

____ 9. I am rarely distracted from my objective.

____ 10. Typically, I want to try more than one approach to problem-solving.

____ 11. Indecision is uncomfortable for me, and I try to determine a course of action as promptly as possible.

____ 12. I resist being committed to a single way of doing things, preferring to defer decisions.

____ 13. I am my best judge and critic.

____ 14. I tend to look to others for evaluation or to compare my work with theirs.

____ 15. I am persistent in addressing difficult tasks.

____ 16. I tend to procrastinate when faced with difficult tasks.

____ 17. I take pride in my intelligent response to challenge.

____ 18. I take pride in my flexible ingenuity in response to challenge.

____ 19. When I'm working and get tired, I summon up the strength to keep at it.

____ 20. When I'm working and I'm tired, I find a stopping point, and quit for a while.

____ 21. I can fairly be called intellectual.

____ 22. I can fairly be called intuitive.

____ 23. Vision, both literally and metaphorically, is characteristic of me.

____ 24. Responsiveness, both literally and metaphorically, is characteristic of me.

____ 25. I genuinely believe that reaching an objective is where the satisfaction lies.

____ 26. I genuinely believe that how I reach an objective is the most important factor in satisfaction.

Now add up the number of time you chose an odd-numbered statement and how many times you chose an even-numbered one. You will almost surely have a mixture. Odd numbers are traits associated with goal-directed learners and the evens best describe process-oriented people. Goal-directed people are like mountain climbers who, after taking care to secure good equipment and maps, pay as little attention as possible to the scenery—it is standing on top they care about. Once they choose a route, they do not consider or much attend to alternatives. Process-oriented folks will climb the same mountain, observing all the details and alternatives, frequently pausing, and often retracing their steps. Both succeed.

In doing the rituals of this book it is wise to keep track of which mode you are in. The goal-directed learner may tend to gloss over important steps in her eagerness to finish. The process-oriented person may tend to wander from the path and lose track of why he's doing the work. Do what you can to trust both your capacity to accomplish difficult challenges and your ability to be flexible and experimental. Be kind to yourself.

Expectations become reality. You know very well that self-fulfilling prophecy is a powerful mechanism. How we visualize coming events has a profound effect on the energies we project, our choices, and our interpretation of outcomes.

Until you know yourself in more than superficial or even intellectual ways, you are making blind choices about your emotions and spirit. Though some of the emotions that probably motivated you to read this book are terribly painful to examine, until you do they will remain untamed and dangerous to your well-being. I've been conscious in designing these rituals to be logical in their sequence. You wouldn't, after all, want a coach who saw you had talent to overmatch you before you had the experience needed for truly challenging competition. In this case, the prize is the rebirth of pleasure, surely a goal worth working systematically to experience.

Ritual Three: A Fresh Vision

Mary's mind had settled into the routine of expecting—visualizing—her life to be lonely after the death of her husband. She was slow to accept invitations, reluctant to volunteer, and less engaged with others, even family members. When she entered therapy and agreed to practice visualizing herself at a dinner party or reading to folks in a nursing home, she became restless. With support, she translated the restlessness into action, and her long isolation began to end. From the following list, choose the terms or sentences that describe your current condition. On the line at the bottom, write a word or brief sentence about what you'd prefer. Don't worry that, at the moment, it seems difficult or unobtainable. Just concentrate on what would be better.

Example: I find it difficult to be around happy people. I want—no, intend—to be one of them.

____ I find it difficult to be around happy people.

____ I am either sleeping way too much and/or can't seem to get rested.

____ Sorrowful thoughts dominate my mind.

____ I am medicating with alcohol, drugs, gambling, sex, or other substances or behavior.

____ I have few or no positive expectations about the future.

____ I feel doomed to misery or lowered function due to my sorrow.

____ I resent people who don't know what grief is.

____ I feel compromised, useless, and/or impotent in directing my life and future.

____ I don't believe in anything anymore.

Here are clear extremes of perception and behavior which are designed to help you identify your position and make the decision to change in hopeful, pleasure-directed ways. It is, after all, your choice as a conscious person to choose your own direction.

All right! Now you know you can generate positive ideas. These can translate into reality as you learn to transform the energy of suffering and sorrow into a hopeful and self-fulfilling prophecy.

Ritual Four: Pairs of Opposites

1. Remember to begin with four-stroke breathing.

2. Below are a series of words and their opposites. Notice the scale.

3. Now put an "X" on the line that shows where your consciousness has been in this time of sorrow.

4. Put an "!" where you intend it to be before long.

Example: 1 X   3   ! 5
*   isolation   engagement*

1_____3_____5
terrified   serene

1_____3_____5
withdrawn   involved

1_____3_____5
reactive   proactive

1_____3_____5
timid   courageous

1_____3_____5
hopeless   hopeful

1_____3_____5
helpless   effective

1_____3_____5
rageful   peaceful

1_____3_____5
constrained   free

1	3	5
resentful		grateful

1	3	5
stuck		moving

1	3	5
restless		rested

1	3	5
aimless		directed

1	3	5
tense		relaxed

1	3	5
unpleasant		companionable

1	3	5
depressed		cheerful

1	3	5
distrustful		confident

1	3	5
sorrowful		joyous

What you have just done is set a direction in your alchemical process of refining and transmuting suffering into creative life. Pleasure is a quietly comprehensive emotion embodying satisfaction, enjoyment, and appreciation. It is this objective you'll need to keep in mind as you do the work of this book. It is a motivating vision. Take a few of those good breaths you have learned how to do and promise yourself that you will become the happy, productive, and wiser person that is your right. You can now see where you are and where you are going, which is a crucial step. If it seems you have far to go, remember the truthful Chinese adage that the longest journey begins with a single step. And you've already started by reading and working this far in the book you're holding.

PART II

The Nature and Source of Suffering

CHAPTER 2

The Nature of Sorrow

MACBETH: *Canst thou not minister to a mind diseas'd,*
pluck from the memory a rooted sorrow,
Raze out the written troubles of the brain,
And with some sweet oblivious antidote
Cleanse the stuff'd bosom of that perilous stuff
Which weights upon the heart?
DOCTOR: *Therein the patient*
Must minister to himself.

—Shakespeare

MacBeth in his despair cried out, as we all do, for something—some medicine or surgery—to ease "that perilous stuff which weights upon the heart." The wise physician responded with the hard truth that MacBeth must heal himself. While this may seem cold, it is really a challenge to gather forces, resources, and vision to care for ourselves. Fortunately, we have examples in life, literature, and history to demonstrate that this daunting prospect is possible: Stephen Hawking, the physicist whose brilliant mind inhabits a wasted, useless body; Franklin Roosevelt, an athlete who governed from a wheelchair; Rose Kennedy, who saw her sons killed, one by one, and soldiered on; Helen Keller who, rendered blind and deaf in infancy, grew to be a luminous spokesperson for courage; Toulouse-Lautrec, a dwarf who created exuberant art. Each of these examples clearly demonstrates the capacity for pleasure: Hawkins has a rowdy sense of humor, Roosevelt loved his dog and to swim, Kennedy gloried in her grandchildren and great-grandchildren, Keller loved travel and flowers. One has only to look at Toulouse-Lautrec's art to feel his pleasure in the female form and in drawing. Earlier, I introduced the Bennett family as they were facing the decline and death of the forty-one-year-old father, Dan. While their personal processes were certainly different from yours, their examples of ritual work will be helpful in showing you what is possible.

Ritual Five: Inspiration

From Dan Bennett's Journal: *I'm supposed to write about someone I admire . . . Gandhi? Yes, but larger than life sized, particularly now when I have no big causes ahead except dying decently. Mark Twain? Yeah, but he got a little bitter at the end. The guy in Tiananmen Square standing in front of the tank? Too close to home. Got it! Zorba the Greek. What a man you were, Zorba! A lot of dumb mistakes based on a passion to experience, to be alive, to engage. Slept with a lot of women. Fought wars. Mined lignite. Played music, danced. What an example, and you died standing up, defying the priests and mourners, angry that there wasn't more life for you. Hey man, I can identify!*

1. Remember to follow the instructions of ritual 1.

2. Let your mind wander to people, alive or dead, in your life, history, or literature, whom you admire or find inspirational. Choose one.

3. Write this person a brief letter (use your journal for this). In the letter, detail what about them gives you hope or guidance. Also acknowledge the difficulties you know that they have endured. Finally, connect the trials they experienced with the behavior and character you admire.

Sorrow is a universal experience, shared by all humankind. We are born weak, unskilled, and dependent. As we mature, we gain physical, emotional, spiritual, and intellectual strengths. We learn to provide for ourselves and we seek mates. We reproduce ourselves and nurture our young. We become elders, teaching by example. We lose powers, and finally, we die. Carl Jung, the great Swiss psychological pioneer, once commented, "To the psychotherapist, an old man who cannot bid farewell to life appears as feeble and sickly as a young man who is unable to embrace it."

At any point in our cycle, however, we are vulnerable to personal extinction. An apparently random accident, war, sickness, a genetic flaw, savage aggression, or a personal choice may interrupt our progression toward a merciful death in old age, potential fulfilled.

At birth, we suffer the loss of security and protection of the womb; later we suffer the loss of our mother's breast and her constant attention as we are displaced by younger siblings or our own need to explore. We have all suffered loss as we involved ourselves with the world. Some of our losses were tangible; others not. If our second-grade teacher made a false accusation of cheating against us, we may have lost our faith in justice. Our best efforts sometimes don't measure up to another's standards. The loss of innocence is the price of experience. In maturity, we suffer the loss of our earlier dreams. We may find that we must abandon our aspirations to save the world. We may darkly suspect we will not have a perfect marriage, achieve a dazzling level of success, or reach enlightenment by forty. The disillusion of failed dreams, the loss of perceived truths, and the recognition of personal limitations are catastrophes that may devastate our optimism and self-esteem.

We are required to transform such losses into a refined awareness that enhances our inner strength and enlarges the means of our accomplishments. Would Ray Charles' piano music be as elegant if he were not blind? Would Mother Teresa's luminous face have shone as brightly in a "safe" convent far from the festering slums of Calcutta? We are bound to follow their examples or regret not only our losses but our inability to use them as alchemical fire.

Loss takes many forms and is most poignantly felt for that which is most dear. We may mourn the lost of "being in love" or of comforting ideas such as "the world is fair." I have wept over the loss of an object—Grandmother's watch—and a place—the house my father and grandfather built and in which I was born—and, of course, people—a son, husband, mother, grandparents, father, friends, brother-in-law, clients, and victims of disasters. The more intimate and valued the idea or person, the greater the fear of loss and the greater the anguish when it occurs. The death of a child wrenches a parent's soul harder than any other personal catastrophe.

Failed relationships, faded youth, destroyed homelands, loss of independence, disillusion with God, lost promises, abandoned talents, spent passions, and deaths of intimates, all carry their baggage of sorrow. When we are bereaved—left alone when someone dear has died—we are sorrowful. Anger, confusion, denial, terror, and despair may invade our hearts. Our feelings will be powerful, perhaps foreign, and will dominate our existence for a while.

Ritual Six: Your Own Experience with Sorrow

From Sylvia Bennett's journal: *I'm supposed to write about a past time of life. I choose mid-childhood.*

Climbing trees
Swinging on ropes
Dangling over the precipice
Then, it was fun.

1. Perform ritual 1.

2. Spend some time remembering scenes from your childhood. Thumbing through a family album is often helpful or talking with someone who "knew you when." Remember the places, people, and events that have stayed in memory. Write a paragraph including a place, a person, and an event that you remember fondly.

3. Read it aloud as you sit alone. Pay attention to your breath, your heartbeat, and emotions.

4. Assess how you were shaped by what you've recalled. If you are settled as to the value of the remembered situation, acknowledge the importance of what was lost as you aged, and how the benefit lives on.

5. Visualize the scene as best you can. Give it thanks. Now, do the important part: say "Goodbye" right out loud. This is doing good grief work. If you cry, that is good—it is cleansing. Give yourself credit for courage.

6. Go the through the same steps regarding your youth.

7. Repeat them for your young adulthood.

8. Depending on your age as you do this work, touch in at each major season already experienced.

Condition or Process?

If we think of our grief as a condition, we live as if being sorrowful, abandoned, or wounded is our identity. We can have a condition for a long time, even a lifetime. Thinking of grief as a condition creates stagnant energy. If we think of grief as a process, we emphasize movement and change—including a beginning, intermediate steps, and hope of resolution of our anguish. Thinking of grief, as a process creates dynamic energy. Love, creativity, grief, and maturation are processes—and pleasure is a proper part of all of them.

Ritual Seven: Stagnant or Moving

Which of the following statements come close to describing your current perspective?

1. I can never get over what has happened.

2. Time heals.

3. My life stopped when my loss occurred.

4. I am trying to understand how to move forward in my life.

5. I see no reason to hope I'll feel better.

6. I want to do something to mark this time of life, so that when I'm older, I'll know I've done as well as I can see how.

7. People should be kind to me because I've suffered so much.

8. People are kind to me because I'm a worthwhile person.

9. I refuse all offers of companionship that are outside my suffering.

10. I am willing to try some new things.

11. I need more attention, effort, and time from others because I can't really take care of myself anymore after what's happened.

12. While I accept and appreciate others' concern for me, my preference is to normalize my life.

13. I make only minimal plans because nothing interests me.

14. I continue to engage with life.

The even-numbered statements are characteristic of a person suffering from a condition. They are devoid of positive anticipation. The odd-numbered ones are descriptive of the attitude of a person engaged with the process of healing, however difficult.

Moving from a Condition to a Process

Suppose you have just discovered you are "stuck" in a condition and you would much rather be "movin' right along" with your life? Simply wanting the change is the beginning. After all, without insight it is impossible to consciously act.

It is usually unsettling for people to realize they have actually been benefiting from being immobilized, but it happens. Rose, Sylvia Bennett's mother, had been widowed a couple of years before Dan's crisis. Rose, a self-described "1940s housewife," was understandably devastated at the closing of her fifty-two-year marriage. Two years later—a long time—she was still unwilling to make new social contacts, finish any of her long-pending craft projects, entertain her family, or go on even short trips. Lack of exercise and poor nutrition were compromising her health. Medical intervention, initiated by Sylvia, had failed to penetrate her immobility.

Friends and family were sympathetic and deeply concerned. They brought food, videos, and offers of outings. Rose was, without planning it, getting a lot of "secondary gain" (unexpected valuable benefits) from her passivity. She had long since quit contributing, but she was receiving attention regularly. In her case, there was a pay off for having a "grief-stricken condition." She was, in her grandson's words, "Pretty soggy. She won't even pick the roses in her garden. She's no fun, and I'm tired to trying to cheer her up. I think she likes being bummed."

Without in any way diminishing the cataclysmic change Ralph's death had brought to her life, Rose was failing to take responsibility for the years she had remaining. Had she had the insight, coupled with the determination, to change, she might have found enjoyment in her life, including the satisfaction of doing service and setting a wholesome example to her grandsons. Rose could have had a much pleasanter life. Ralph would have applauded.

Insight, determination, and vision are the keys to progress in any process of sorrow. You must see the truth of being stuck, make up your mind to use all your resources (people, places, activities) to "rejoin the living," and hold a mental picture of change. Hope, of course, is critical. In the following ritual, put out some effort to climbing out of your hole and taking a new look at the landscape.

Ritual Eight: Moving Energy

A piece of coal was formed millions of years ago. It is mined and shipped, with tons of other coal, toward a smelter. But somehow it is dropped at the side of a railroad track. A little boy, Todd, is exploring in a place he knows may be dangerous, but since the railroad track crosses the canyon that holds a river, he has decided to cross over and see what is on the other side. Just as he starts across, he sees the lump of coal and puts it in his pocket.

He goes on across safely and finds a big boulder near the other side. Proud of himself for daring the walk, he writes with the coal on the huge stone: "Todd was here". Later, when he tells his friends about the daring thing he did, they don't believe him. So he takes them on a trip with him and shows them the evidence of his name. Conclusion: Even energy long held in suspension (like that which was in the coal) can be activated in my life.

1. It is very important that you return to and practice ritual 1 at this time for it is a vivid way of recognizing your own power to move your energy.

2. Below are some images of stagnant, frozen, broken, or immobilized energy. Choose several images, then write a small story or vignette, like the one above, that illustrates the energy not only moving but accomplishing something desirable in the way of usefulness or beauty. Draw a conclusion about what that might mean in your life.

    ____ Glacier as it reaches the sea

    ____ Dead tree in a forest

    ____ Broken bicycle

    ____ Shelf of long unopened books

_____ Swamp

_____ Sleeping Beauty

_____ Abandoned house

_____ Drifting lifeboat

3. Even if drawing isn't your long suit, make a sketch illustrating each of the vignettes you have written and include some representation of yourself as a participant.

Manifestations of Sorrow

We experience degrees of suffering, but the quality of the experience differs only in the details of time, intensity, and potential learning. A burnt fingertip is of the same quality as a terrible scald. The nature of the burned flesh differs only in how deep, how broad, and where on the body it occurs. The loss of a beloved animal is not less real, not less dreadful, not less important than the loss of a person, though it's not the same. What differs is that we have generally built our lives around a parent, partner, or spouse with all the complexity of intermeshed personalities, experiences, and plans over time. We may have unfinished business in the form of words unsaid, grievances unresolved, or actions deferred. With the animal, this is rarely true—but the nature of the pain is parallel.

Ritual Nine: Your Experiences of Loss

Michael Bennett's essay: *I remember camping with Dad and Granddad. We ate marshmallows for breakfast on lumpy oatmeal. A bear knocked the lid off the garbage can and spread fish guts all over. The next year Granddad died, and we never went back to the lake, but sometimes I smell fish stuff when I eat marshmallows.*

1. Perform ritual 1.

2. Think about the places you have enjoyed and felt at home. They may be big areas, like the desert, or as snug as a playhouse in a tree. Choose one that is no longer accessible to you. Write a descriptive paragraph about what it meant to you and how it influences you today.

3. Remember an activity you once enjoyed, but can no longer participate in. Write a descriptive paragraph about what it meant to you and how it influences you today.

4. Remember an object and go through the same steps.

5. Remember a person and do the same thing.

6. Now ask yourself, "Since I have this memory and understand its importance in my life, what have I learned about loss?"

The Wounded Healer

The theme of "the wounded healer" is found in all traditions. The idea is this: It is through suffering that we understand the value and importance of life and enhance our spiritual depth. Once wounded, we never again take for granted the joy of spring daffodils, a child's laughter, the creative surge, a gentle touch, or any other sweet gift of living consciously. The wounded healer may function in the community as an example: the gifted woodworker operating from a wheelchair or the mother of the child killed by random gunfire working for violence-abatement programs. Such people, who have healed and mobilized their power, show us that it can be done.

At first you may believe the task is impossible, that you are inadequate, that nothing really matters anyway. Such thinking is toxic and robs you of hope. Loss of hope is lethal to vitality. Better we reframe our suffering to see it as a ladder. Each rung ascended from the pit of despondency provides a better perspective and greater appreciation for each breath taken.

If you will simply observe, there are examples all around, of those who have experienced bereavement, illness, displacement, and other losses. These people have grieved but have also arisen to live enhanced lives of creativity, service, and happiness. They demonstrate that pleasure is possible, even after such a massive challenge.

Ritual Ten: Looking for Teachers

From Dan Bennett's journal: *My father was the best and the worst teacher of my life. He gave me woodworking tools along with so many cautions not to cut myself that I didn't want to try. He showed me what a rigid mind-set can do to block learning, but he also taught me to sing out loud . . . from the belly. He showed me honor and principle, but not empathy. It took Sylvia to really drive that home.*

In your life, you have known many people. Some have had what look like "hard lives" and others seem to slide along with fewer losses. There is an old, bitter joke about how anyone can be an example, it's just that some are bad ones. Choose someone you think is a good example of surviving the "School of Hard Knocks." This will be a person who, consciously or not, has reacted to grief as a process to be experienced. Spend some time reflecting on what you know of their lives. Try to imagine how they made the steps in their grief process from hurt to example. If you know them well enough, have a conversation and ask how they accomplished their changes. Write a summary of your thinking.

Now consider who might function as a good example of someone immersed in a grief condition, someone assuming the identity of a suffering person. Not someone in the throes of a recent loss, but a person who has retained this identity over time. Pay attention to how they reinforce their circular, stagnant thinking. What do they say, how do they behave in order to stay in the role? How does staying stuck seem to benefit them? Do they get a lot of solicitous attention? Do they justify doing nothing this way? What have they given up in life? Now do what you can to understand how they are keeping themselves from rejoining life.

Did you remember to do ritual 1 before beginning? If not, do your best to fix it in memory as the proper support to give yourself in this challenging work. Perform ritual 1, now. It'll feel good.

The Emotions Associated with Sorrow

From Sylvia's journal:

Buttons missing off Mike's shirt
Pickets falling off the fence
Hornworms in the tomatoes
Dan's side of the bed, empty. Sound of vomiting
Trying not to hear
Trying not to know.
Be a brave wife
Be a good nurse
Howling, inside.

Gray hair at my temple
Mold on the cottage cheese
In the dirty refrigerator
Dust insidiously intrudes
Under our king-size bed.

Things uncompleted
Work not finished
Loopholes in the contract
Holes in my sweater sleeve
Everything is unraveling.

The source of sorrow is loss. The yin-yang parallel of the sweetness of love is paired with the bitterness of loss. Each of us comes to points in our lives when something we treasure is taken from us. We may not even have known its value before it was gone. How we react will depend on our own natures, the importance of the person, object, creature, place, process, or position no longer accessible to us, and to the wisdom of those around us.

Ritual Eleven: Losses

Perform ritual 1.

In the list below, check those items that you have experienced as losses. On the line or in your journal, give yourself a rating on how well you have processed this loss. Give yourself a 1 if you feel the loss is still raw and hurtfully influencing your life today. Give yourself a 5 if you feel complete with your acceptance and are not suffering. In-between numbers indicate your progress. Be generous with yourself but honest as well. The point of this is to know where to concentrate your attention in the rituals to follow. If someone or something important has been omitted, be sure to add that loss to your list.

Example: Childhood home____4____

____ Spouse ____

____ Mother ____

____ Father ____

____ Grandmothers ____

_____ Grandfathers _____

_____ Child _____

_____ Close relatives _____

_____ Close friends or colleagues _____

_____ Loved animals _____

_____ Places: home(s) and geographical areas _____

_____ Important physical talents and/or mental abilities from another time of life. List them specifically.

_____ _____

_____ _____

_____ Dreams _____

_____ Illusions _____

_____ Trust _____

_____ Objects: things of great significance to you _____

_____ Status, position, or role _____

List other losses that you have either moved through to wholesome acceptance and accommodation or which are still inhibiting and distorting your life.

_____ _____

_____ _____

The Elements of Sorrow

Sorrow is no single thing: it comes in degrees or increments and is usually an amalgam of several emotions. My sorrow of watching the wanton destruction of Earth is composed of fear for the future, anger at the greedy stupidity fueling it, and soul-deep mourning for the creatures, places, and processes lost. This sorrow motivates me to resist in every way I can the forces killing Earth. This, in turn, addresses the misery of feeling impotent and complicit by channeling my anger into direct resistance, which often yields heartening gains. Planting cedar trees on hills that have been clear-cut into desolation is a requiem for fallen giants and a gesture of trust to the future. It transforms stagnant energy into hopeful action.

Anger is a call for action. It is fueled by adrenaline in the "fight-or-flight" response. Anger turned inward manifests as depression and self-destructive behaviors. Some depressions, of course, are biochemical in nature or are resultant of repressed traumas. This is a separate topic not addressed in this book.

The anger of being thwarted and offended is what incites me to resist destructive forces. Anger is not all fist-shaking and raging; it is very useful in accomplishing change. Mohandas Gandhi's life of courageous noncompliance to oppression provided a path for his angry sorrow at the brutal British rule and shrewdly mobilized others to create a new nation.

The sorrow Sylvia Bennett expressed in her poem was one of incredulous recognition that her life, in all its pleasant, familiar particulars, was being distorted and was "unraveling." Her confused recognition of the situation is part of the sorrow complex. Later, in a different mood, she wrote:

> *Scared of living*
> *Scared of dying*
> *Scared of the kids*
> *Scared of myself*
> *Scared of pain*
> *Scared of winter*
> *Scared of everything.*
>
> *Scared of Dan*
> *Scared for Dan*
> *Scared God got lost in the smog*
> *Scared I'll wake up*
> *And another day'll be gone.*

Fear often comes when we feel a lack of control, and it, too, is a part of the complex called sorrow. Fear is negative anticipation without recognition that alternative ways of thinking exist. This is an important concept. Fear is telling ourselves scary stories, visualizing the worst, and imaging catastrophe. In Sylvia's circumstances, there is a sense of powerlessness and of things being beyond her control—"God got lost in the smog."

One alternative to fear is denial, which is somehow convincing ourselves that the loss we are grappling with "can't happen" or has little meaning. The problem with this defense is that it blunts truth and effectively makes creative action or thought impossible—all without affirming life. I've heard clients faced with serious surgery declare that "it isn't anything" or known them to "put on a happy face" rather than seek the comfort of those they love. This sort of thing is like wallpapering over the cockroaches: the damn things keep moving! It is only when we can recognize our circumstances that we can take charge of our thoughts, visions, stories, and actions.

Fear that because one child has died in a family, all the remaining ones are in heightened danger is a common, understandable response. However, it will distort the relationships without effectively providing any margin of security. When the energy of the fear is transformed into appreciation of those still living and is coupled with the determination that they will be supported to experience life fully (rather than being coccooned in a parent's bundle of anxiety), then fear fades. Impotence is the sense of powerlessness, of the inability to influence events, of being a spectator in a situation about which you deeply care. It is particularly galling if you have been a person able to take charge, make things happen, manage well.

We feel fear when we are unable to control those things that matter bone-deep, when we know ourselves to be impotent. Even though control is often an illusion—we didn't have control or the initial loss wouldn't have occurred—it's still frightening to recognize our impotence in these heart-felt matters.

Abandonment is probably the first and most terrifying feeling most people experience. I once saw a two-year-old happily wandering the aisle of the grocery store while her mother shopped. At one point, the mother went around a counter, and the child could no longer see her. The panicked screaming for "Mama!" mobilized every adult within earshot, for we all knew what it was to be left behind and not know what to do. Sadly, we all know that feeling from other losses.

The "it's not fair" factor can be one of the toughest. Where we perceive injustice, as in the death of a promising child in an accident with a drunk driver, we are doubly outraged—not only at the loss, but at the unfairness. We may shake our fist at the sky and declare that God is dead, turn cynical and trust nothing, or somehow come to accept that how and to what end such tragedies occur is momentarily veiled from us.

Confusion ("What am I to do?" or "Why me?") is a predictable part of sorrow. It is the nature of humankind to be curious, ask questions, explore, generate ideas, invent, master skills, develop strategies, and bring order to thinking. When loss occurs, we are confused because it "doesn't make sense," or, even worse, "things are out of control."

Chaos is the ultimate confusion. No column adds up the same twice, predictability is fugitive, and logic is suspended. We, who are so clever and well-organized, are lost to our familiar ways of thinking or feeling. All is disrupted. Ultimately, if we are fortunate and diligent, we discover it is out of chaos that creation is born. Sorrow can give birth to a refreshed appreciation of life, positively motivated action, and enriched spiritual depth. There are tools for this and you will be finding them in the rituals ahead.

Ritual Twelve: The Components of Sorrow

1. You know now which ritual to do first. Prepare yourself for the worthwhile effort of identifying the emotions disturbing you.

2. Below is a substantial list of common emotional/physical manifestations of sorrow. Check the ones that are present in your life at this time.

3. In your journal, write a few sentences about how you experience each of them.

   Examples: If you check "Anger": *I feel resentment when I see happy couples out together.* Someday soon, I will be glad to witness people enjoying each other.

   Or: My anger is all over the place. Just having a hard time opening a box of cereal infuriates me. It won't be long until I have a better grip on my emotions and will laugh at such a little frustration.

4. Here's a challenge: after each of the sentences in step number 3, write an alternative sentence that shows another, pleasurable possibility.

   ____ Fear or anxiety.

   ____ Fatigue or exhaustion beyond what is expected from my activities.

   ____ Confusion to the point where I don't feel efficient or able to conduct my life as I once did.

   ____ Helplessness. "There is nothing I can do . . ."

   ____ Guilt. I feel responsible for what has happened or feel ungrateful for my blessings.

   ____ Shame. I am humiliated or feel totally unworthy of the good things coming my way.

   ____ Sadness. My mood is almost entirely dark, little amuses or intrigues me.

   ____ Hate. I have the impulse to do harm to another or take revenge.

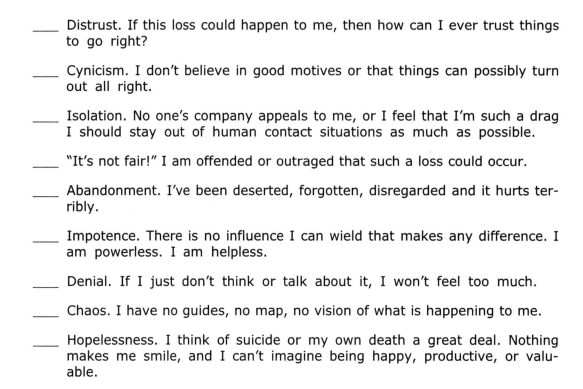

____ Distrust. If this loss could happen to me, then how can I ever trust things to go right?

____ Cynicism. I don't believe in good motives or that things can possibly turn out all right.

____ Isolation. No one's company appeals to me, or I feel that I'm such a drag I should stay out of human contact situations as much as possible.

____ "It's not fair!" I am offended or outraged that such a loss could occur.

____ Abandonment. I've been deserted, forgotten, disregarded and it hurts terribly.

____ Impotence. There is no influence I can wield that makes any difference. I am powerless. I am helpless.

____ Denial. If I just don't think or talk about it, I won't feel too much.

____ Chaos. I have no guides, no map, no vision of what is happening to me.

____ Hopelessness. I think of suicide or my own death a great deal. Nothing makes me smile, and I can't imagine being happy, productive, or valuable.

The Elements of Pleasure

Just as sorrow is not a one-component, one-intensity emotion, neither is pleasure. I have felt satisfaction at things as different as looking at my pantry shelves and counting the eighty jars of salsa I've just canned and admiring a picture of my granddaughter all tricked out in a fancy horse-riding outfit. Enjoyment comes from events as varied and disparate as finding the first trillium of spring under a hemlock tree to an evening of banter with a quick-witted companion. There is pleasure in planning a trip, getting the linen closet straightened out, and in signing a book contract—all of which seem like accomplishments to me. Appreciation of nature, friends, activities, and places often fills me with pleasure. In my life, pleasure has segued into happiness at creative ventures, in relationships, and in the insights that have allowed me to alter my life in the direction of my own choice.

Recognize that the list you have made is another measure of recovery. Self-knowledge is the foundation for change, growth, and fulfillment. Give yourself some rest, some exercise, some company: You've made a brave step and deserve reward.

CHAPTER 3

The Alchemy of Hope

Hope is the thing with feathers
That perches in the soul
And sings the tune without the words
And never stops at all.

And sweetest in the gale is heard;
And sore must be the storm
That could abash the little bird
That kept so many warm.

I've heard it in the chillest land
And on the strangest sea,
Yet never in extremity
It asked a crumb of me.

—Emily Dickinson

What is this "thing with feathers" called hope? It is the precious, energizing complex of emotions and thought that protects you from despairing at the disappointments, setbacks, and losses that life inevitably presents. When you are hope-*full* you are able to formulate and execute ideas, reach out for and accept touch, flex with challenge, and sense existence as a privilege. You are full, active, and juicy. Pleasure comes easily. In the hope-*less* periods of life you are emotionally and intellectually blunted, battered, unresponsive. You experience yourself as drained, empty.

How do you get from this present misery to bright hope? To answer that crucial question requires discussion of an ancient science/philosophy: alchemy.

Alchemy

The terrible fire of grief is an energetic furnace, refining character, personality, intellect, and soul. It is a catalyst for creation. What is created may be dreadful—a distorted, unapproachable monument to despair—or a distillation of experience that is wholesome, useful, bright, and even wise. As Jung said so clearly, "There is no birth of consciousness without pain."

The alchemist of antiquity was absorbed in the elusive task of transmuting lead to gold or pig offal to pearls. While alchemy may conjure up images of sorcerers, boiling cauldrons, and dark, medieval laboratories, alchemy was actually a sophisticated spiritual discipline. Painstaking experimentation was conducted with a meditative attunement to the chemical changes being produced.

Transformations in physical matter corresponded with changes in consciousness and were meticulously devised to foster healing and spiritual development. To give a measure of the status of alchemy, Leonardo da Vinci was a practicing alchemist, and Sir Isaac Newton had a laboratory designated for alchemical research. In this section of the book, I use the ancient tradition of alchemy as a metaphor for transmuting anguish and sorrow into wisdom, creativity, and pleasure.

Life presents us with repeated opportunities to take "base" or common events—disillusion, outrage, grief—and shape them to our benefit or detriment. The profound emotions associated with deep loss may affect the mourner's character in ways that are devastating and destructive, or they may open the heart to deeper truths than have ever before been glimpsed.

The principle of transformation is a central concern of philosophy, mythology, and psychotherapy. All religions portray some image of salvation or positive change at the core of their message to the world. The politician, preacher, or counselor who extinguishes optimism fails. To be effective, teachers and leaders must offer hope for a different, more desirable future.

Whether we turn frogs into princes, watch acorns become oaks, or weave straw into baskets, each of us lives daily with examples of energy changing into new forms. Of course, it's also possible to imagine princes becoming tyrants, ancient oaks falling to a woodsman's ax, and baskets crushed under heavy loads. What is not possible is for life to advance unaltered. The only thing that seems certain is eternal change.

The Need for a Personal Philosopher's Stone

The alchemists of medieval times attempted to create or discover a "philosopher's stone," a chemical preparation with the power of transmuting base metals into gold. All human beings need a personal philosopher's stone—its name is hope. Hope is the alchemical ingredient required by the psyche if life's base experiences are to be transmuted into a creative response. Without hope, problems go unsolved, systems of law, religion, and philosophy lose their meaning, and the burden of life becomes intolerable. Without hope, the instinct for survival, which keeps us stubbornly resisting death, weakens.

The medieval alchemist was himself a vital part of his "noble experiment." His enlightened attitude and full-hearted devotion to the task were considered essential to the process. The alchemist had to responsibly direct personal energy to be capable of orchestrating the miracle of metamorphosis.

Today, all men and women are their own alchemists. We are presented daily with opportunities for transmuting the tests and tribulations of life into meaning, wisdom, joy, and compassion. We each need to create from our experiences in life a personal philosopher's stone—hope—in order to spark the alchemical transformation of loss into emotional growth and creative action.

To develop, sustain, or rebuild hope, we must nurture a core of optimism and see ourselves as capable of learning, even in the midst of daunting challenges. We must cultivate a personal mythology that affirms our ability to work through our despair and find fresh meaning. Hope grows out of the experience and practice of making life-supporting choices. We can train ourselves to incubate trust in the positive powers of existence. In the following pages you will be developing mental habits that support hope, and you will learn how to deal more effectively with elements of your inner life that defeat it. Hope—the philosopher's stone—is the irreplaceable catalyst in the alchemy of transmuting grief and agony into wisdom and creativity.

Loss as Alchemical Fire

In addition to base material, the philosopher's stone, and a worthy practitioner, alchemy has another essential element: fire. Fire cleanses, purifies, alters, and prepares the base material. Literally *nothing* leaves the fire unaltered by the exposure.

Sorrow and anguish are the elements of grief. In the alchemy of transmuting grief to creativity, sorrow is the base material to be transformed and anguish is the flame. Their combustion causes unspeakable pain, tests endurance, challenges assumptions, and refines us. When we add hope to the mixture, our response to disaster becomes immeasurably more creative.

For myself, as a person who has walked this road before you, I have grown in my capacity to forgive myself my blemishes and inadequacies, to "play my strengths," and to savor everything good or stimulating that comes my way. What was precious has become more dear, and what is foolish has, to some extent, been dropped. I not only actively seek, but frequently experience, pleasure. This is part of my own ongoing refinement.

That I am incomplete, immature and flawed is unmistakable—but I do not imagine my worst traits following me, unaltered, to my grave. I have come to believe that change is inevitable, and that I have the responsibility and opportunity to direct much of that change. I am, in Carl Rogers' memorable use of the term, "becoming." I am becoming more complete, more mature, more in touch with the infinite as I live. This is my self-defined purpose in life. It is my affirmation and my mantra.

Resurgent vitality, the desire to be of service, a capacity to enjoy, a willingness to commit to and receive from others, delight and fun, the enjoyment of nature, an ability to plan and persevere, and a clear sense of purpose in living—all these are the signs to watch for in charting your progress through the alchemical flames of grief. Each step in refining creative living from the chaos of misery is to be celebrated as it occurs. You are a marvelously resilient organism.

You have virtually unlimited avenues for your expressive work and for finding pleasure. You have your body, with all your vital sensory gifts—movement, touch, sound, and vision. You have innate intelligence and the ability to study, to gain understanding, and to seek wisdom. You have your emotions—ranging from apathy and alienation to excitement, love, and rapture. You have your deep connection with the infinite or divine, however you conceive it to be. You are equipped to live, learn, and evolve.

If you choose to break free of stagnant energy, to cultivate hope rather than live with dreary images, you have passed a critical test for moving on in your life to greater creativity, fulfillment, and spiritual awareness.

The choice is yours. Blessings.

Ritual Thirteen: Defining an Intention

From Sylvia's journal: *Damn Peg! It isn't enough that I keep putting one foot ahead of the other. No! I'm supposed to think about "what I intend to do with my energy, with my life." She's right, but man! It's hard!*

I intend to survive this. I don't entirely want to because I don't trust my own resources, but the reality is, I have two sons. I intend to see that they have every opportunity to be the kind of men that Dan and I have dreamed of. Sure, they'll be scarred, but I can work to keep that wound from being a festering ulcer. I intend to be normal, and if that means being bitchy or sniveling some of the time, so what! I'm royally pissed off, and I intend to figure out what to do with the energy. I intend to behave like an honest, loving adult. But sometimes I will be a child, like I am now inside. I intend to keep on loving and hollering and writing and mothering and trying. And I intend to eventually laugh out loud again.

Love's intention is to exist and perpetuate itself.

1. Intentions are templates, just like dress patterns or the cardboard mock-ups used for cutting carpet, metal, or wood. They help us define our choices and assemble the pieces into pleasing, useful products.

2. Write a paragraph on your intentions for your intellectual life. It might include books to read, classes to take, gatherings to attend.

3. Write a paragraph on your intentions for your emotional well-being. Include fun and creative expression.

4. Write a paragraph on your intentions for your physical well-being.

5. Write a paragraph on your intentions for your social life, including both family and friends.

6. Write a paragraph on your intentions for the service you plan to give to others.

7. Write a paragraph on your intentions for your spiritual life.

8. Finish up with a note of encouragement to yourself, such as you'd send to a good friend who is awakening from sorrow into creative living.

9. Did you remember to do your four-stroke breathing ritual to start? Hope so! If not, do it now as a refreshing reward for all this work.

The Bennetts Creatively Address Sorrow

As they faced the enormous change that Dan's failing health and coming death forced upon them, the Bennetts went through many stages of disbelief, resentment, bargaining, and struggle. Because they were good-willed, essentially happy, and certainly creative people, a deepened perspective on life began emerging. Sylvia, the wife and poet, wrote a piece different in tone from her earlier ones.

There is mercy in drenching rain
Washing the dust and dog crap away,
Leaving trees and city freshly cleansed.
There is mercy in a raging storm
Ravaging the coast and removing all
The sailors' wine bottles and Twinkie wrappers.
There is mercy in ripping, rending pain
In the agony of separation and unanswerable questions
Removing all the etiquette, false smiles, and
Untried, politic assumptions about reality,
Leaving truth and love and laughter and God in its wake.

Michael, the twelve-year-old, wrote an essay, at my behest, that he gave Dan.

My Dad
by Michael Tyrone Bennett

My dad has red hair, like me. He is a good sailor and wins lots of races. When I grow up, I'll get a bigger boat than the Good Times *and sail around the world to Fiji and Borneo, like he wants to do. My dad eats the potato chips and then says he doesn't know what happened to them. When I was little, he used to take baths with me and we'd play boats. He told me never to blow bubbles in the bath water when Mom was around. He's lots of fun to build models with. My dad wants me to do good in school. I'm bored in school, so I don't do too much work. I'd rather play basketball.*

My dad has cancer, and he has to spend a lot of time in bed. He gets shots for pain at night, and then he snores. I like to hear him snore because I know he isn't hurting.

My dad knows how to talk to kids, and he does it all day at his work. Once a kid my age was doing bad things, like smoking dope and stealing. After he talked to my dad, he got better, and his parents got better, too. I heard Dad talking to Mom about it when they thought I was watching TV.

My dad spanked me for starting up the car without permission. I think he was scared. So was I. I'm glad I have the dad I have.

The End

I included these touching personal pieces by Sylvia and Michael Bennett as examples of expressive grief work. The pain is evident, the relationship is clear. In self-defining this way, both people deepened self-understanding and emptied out a measure of grief. In "making space" this way, there is room and energy for making choices and having experiences that positively advance life. You will soon have the opportunity to perform a ritual that may startle you into a fresh awareness of the balance within you. Remember, where there is deep pain, there is also the potential for genuine gratification.

Transforming Energy: Creating Life

Energy can be neither created nor destroyed. It may, however, be stagnant, misdirected, unrecognized, or unruly. Negative energy tarnishes hope and can overwhelm us. Negative energy is often directed toward revenge or other ultimately self-destructive activities.

At some level, each of us is aware of hidden and destructive forces, the unclaimed and disowned parts of ourselves that Jung referred to as "the shadow." The shadow sabotages our best efforts and whispers messages of destruction that are at odds with our finest aspirations. The shadow is pure energy, often flowing in directions inimical to the well-being of ourselves and others. The sorrowing person does well to focus energy on the parts of life that nurture and heal while being wary of the seductions of the shadow.

We have all known people whom we found draining. As a psychotherapist, I have worked with people who wanted so much from me that I felt as if my veins were open and my vitality was draining out of me. The very next client, however, may have been presenting a parallel problem, yet was so determined and actively engaged in the healing task that I came away uplifted and excited.

The first kind of client is passive and looks to me for change. I must guard against the grandiose and foolish temptation to believe that I can be the magician he or she is seeking.

When I work with a vital client, we enter the fire together, each shielded by our life-experience, each cooperating with the other, each trusting the other's good will. A mutually enriching process is underway. The changes are clearly for the client to make, though I will be enriched and altered by entering her or his fire, even as a guide.

There is an old Irish saying, "The same fire that melts the wax hardens the steel." We must each choose whether to be flabby, quickly consumed wax, or resilient, tempered steel. Further, the alchemical grief furnace may produce the gold of empathy, spirituality, maturity, pleasure, and creative expression. This treasure is refined from common sorrow.

To speak of "common sorrow" is not to suggest that it is easier to bear—or less profound—because it is a universal human experience. That would be like saying that war is banal because of its commonality, or that the havoc wrought on Earth's living body is trivial because of its pervasiveness. The abscess in your jaw hurts no whit less because your brother has one, too. Just as I cannot adequately describe the flavor licorice, the color amber, or the sound of a waterfall, there is no way to make sense of a comparison between your pain and mine. Neither is there a yardstick to measure which of us is the more sorrowful. Nor does it matter. We have each stumbled into the searing fire and must endure and transcend, comforting one another as best we can. Sorrow is our common ground

Casualties of grief are those sad people overwhelmed by despair who have not made choices leading them to cleansing and refinement. The common feature among them is unremitting anguish. They build, consciously or not, a bitter memorial to their dead loved ones, lost causes, abandoned hopes. The memorial is made of pain, anger, desolation, abandonment, resistance, and stagnant energy. They worship at this shrine, giving up their own lives to twist memories into the emotional equivalent of paper flowers in "everlasting" funeral wreaths. They see no path, no hope, no reason to stir themselves. I feel compassion for their grief and am restless for them to be up and about, growing into the next phase of their lives

Modern people are no different from their ancestors in needing guiding myths to provide frameworks for leading purposeful lives. Myths are not simply comforting (or terrifying) stories; they are the *result* and expression of deep, often wordless experience. A *numinous* moment is one that connects us with parts of ourselves ordinarily hidden. We may experience blinding insight, firm inner instruction, or a "knowingness" that surpasses any previous convictions. When we have had such an opening of consciousness, we are forever changed. This sort of awakening brings us to an unassailable understanding that there is reason and purpose in our existence. How this purpose is revealed, how we describe its origins and power, and how sturdily we live our intentions is an individual matter.

When I was working with the Bennett family, Sylvia was clearly in need of a radical change of consciousness. The following is an excerpt from her journal.

From Sylvia's Journal—Late November: *Just back from my vision quest. Peg suggested that since so much depends on me and greater challenges are certainly ahead, I needed to take some time out and regroup. She had to talk me into it. Taking time for myself just seemed too selfish, and besides, it meant losing some of the little time I have left with Dan. Finally, she gave me a book that shows how modern people can do something similar to tribal custom. That is, go apart, fast, and do a ritual seeking guidance. The idea caught my imagination, and God knows, I need something to sustain me. The kids' needs, Mom falling to pieces, Dan's folks coming, and watching Dan fade are overwhelming. So, I did it.*

Took my tent, sleeping bag, ground cloth, water supply, warm clothes, and first-aid kit. That's all (besides some emergency food in the car). Thankful for all the primitive camping experience I've had with Dan, I drove out into the Anza-Borrego Desert looking for the right spot.

I was pretty scared. I've never really been alone, and there is a whole lot of stuff stirred up in me now. Took a dirt side road that seemed lonely. The plan was for me to fast for three days and just spend time alone in nature. I was to make up a ritual that would help me feel part of the place and remain open to any guidance that came my way. Pretty radical. No books, no journal, no writing material, no toys. Just me and the desert. I was on my own resources. Part of a vision quest is the presence of real, genuine, danger. Meeting the challenge.

I was hungry only the first day. Then I got fascinated with all the detail around me: rocks, sand, skyline, creosote bushes. I saw a tarantula loping along looking for bugs or whatever they eat. Was surprised at its beauty—not threatening at all. As luck would have it, the canyon faced east, so the sun woke me. I slept out on the ground, even though I knew it wasn't smart, what with snakes and scorpions around. I couldn't resist the wide-open, star-spangled sky. I could feel the weight of the sickroom falling off me with every breath of the cool, clean air.

Things began to feel different about the middle of the second day. The sky is so big! The landscape so dramatic! I felt small, yet part of it. I was surviving—probably because it was November, not August. I began to really feel part of it. Like, if I died, I'd dry out. The ants and maybe buzzards would eat me, and it would be all right. I can't really explain. The desert is so harsh, so beautiful, so clean that dying just seems like part of it, but so does life. I noticed some little, tiny leaves on the underside of the mesquite. Gray, oily little guys, but alive and keeping the plant going. I sort of felt like one of those little leaves.

Made a ring out of stones I dug up and hauled. Wrecked my hands, but I didn't care. It was about eight feet across and took (I counted) three hundred seventy nine rocks, rough, white stones with veins of quartz (I think). Found four extra-big ones and almost ruptured myself getting them into position at (I think) the four cardinal points of the compass. Wished I'd brought matches, so I could have a little fire in the middle. Found a piece of broken glass and tried to focus a ray on some dry twigs, but no luck. Fire eluded me.

Wasn't satisfied with just the stone ring, so I hunted around until I found some colored dirt, a rusty red and a yellow ochre. It took me awhile, but I dug enough from the wall of a wash to make a couple of piles the size of basketballs. I looked at my stained hands and broken nails. As if I were reenacting a tribal memory, I carefully smoothed the coarse sand around the altar and made three concentric rings, alternating the red and ochre dirt. The contrast was beautiful, at least to my eye. I found a skull—I'm pretty sure it was a rabbit—white and kind of translucent, but powdery dry. I put it on the center of the altar rock. For a while I sat and couldn't think what else to do. I was plenty tired and had probably been working on my ritual circle for four or five hours. I drank some water, which tasted delicious. I didn't want food.

Finally, remembered what Peg told me about chanting. Seems that primitive people used to achieve altered states of consciousness. Something in the rhythm, sustained effort, maybe hyperventilation, is hypnotic and leads to changes in metabolism and thus consciousness. Kind of self-conscious at first (though there probably wasn't anyone within fifty miles of my camp), I began. Somehow the traditional "Om" seemed too Oriental for the place, so I just made some weird wavering sounds, experimenting. Felt really odd at first. Then I began to move around the colored circles, inside the stone ring, in a clockwise direction. I decided my clothes were in my way, so I took them off even though the air was probably close to forty degrees. I even took off my shoes, taking my chances with thorns and creatures. This seemed to help, and I really got into it and went on and on. Round and round the circle I went, sometimes bending low, other times prancing and lifting my arms. My breasts swayed, and I could feel my hips jouncing as I danced with my shadow for a long time, almost mesmerized. The air on my skin was like menthol, and even though it was pretty cold, I soon had sweat running down my ribs. I almost never sweat and usually think of it as unpleasant, but there in the desert it felt good. I even liked the smell of it, something new for me.

The exercise felt good, and I set up such a rhythm that I was somehow transported and actually forgot I was the one making the sound. Felt exhilarated for a while, then dizzy, disoriented, then finally I think I tranced out. It was then I had the vision, or the dream, or hallucination, whatever it was. When I woke up, at first I couldn't remember where I was or when I stopped dancing or chanting. My legs ached, and I was chilled through, lying there on the sand in front of my little altar. But most important was the vision.

It was if the rabbit skull got bigger and bigger, until it filled the whole sky. It was shiny white and light went in through the eye sockets so I could see the skull sutures, and the pores in the bone. I was afraid and crouched down, trying to be small. I could tell it wasn't doing any good, so I stood up and walked toward it. I went inside the skull through the open area under the cheek sinus and found I was in a room lit with translucent light and filled with a strange booming, whistling sound. It took me awhile to realize that the sound was my own heartbeat and breathing. I was filled with wonder and said, out loud, "What am I to do?" I didn't think about it. I just said it.

In the next moment, I was filled with the most wonderful sense of—I don't know the right word—safety, maybe, or rightness. Like I was absolutely protected, and I was right in what I was doing. No cares, no bad anticipations, no fear, no questions. What was, was, and that was proper. The words don't describe the feeling. I stayed in the skull a long time, and it was like a womb or heaven or something like that. I just knew that things were as they should be, and that I was as I should be, and there wasn't any conflict or problem. I wish I could describe it better, but the feeling was so strong that I can bring it back anytime I just quiet myself by taking deep breaths and focusing inward. This probably sounds—or is—crazy, but I know it's real. Awful as objective reality is, with Dan dying and the world turning upside down, the paradox is that deep within, all is as it should be.

A Spiritual Context

Such numinous experiences can offer a sense that "something" is in charge and gives meaning to the most profound losses. So may religious consolation. Whether we call to "God," "Goddess," "the Tao," "the Natural Order," "the Transcendent," it is a power larger than our minds can grasp. We are comforted in our isolation, even as we grieve. The sense that "everything happens for a purpose" or is "part of a plan"—even though the pattern or purpose is hidden from us—offers solace and helps to bring order to the disorienting confusion.

The crises of life strip us of our conventions, platitudes, and avoidance, either facing us cruelly with our spiritual poverty or leading us into a deeper sense of our connection with all creation. Bereavement is both a ripping away of denial and an endowment of opportunity to connect with a deep wisdom. We need to trust in a larger plan. Whether that trust grows out of religious beliefs tempered by Job-like faith, or whether it is earned in a creative engagement with the trials of life, it is of immeasurable benefit in facing and transforming the agony of grief.

If you have a clear set of beliefs and practices within established religious institutions, you have a context for numinosity: the scriptures of the Buddhist, Christian, Jewish, Hindu, Muslim, and many other belief systems are compilations of such events. If you're not affiliated with a formal system of belief, you will have to seek your own experience to mature spiritually, or you may choose to be entirely rational, disavowing any validity to the idea of a transcendence participating in your life. Trust is a personal thing.

This is not a book promoting a particular spiritual or religious perspective. These are intimate matters: choosing, experiencing, or inviting numinous experience or cultivating a sense of the sacred. The *how* of explanation of these phenomena is outside my scope and intention in describing and supporting openness in healing sorrow. I have dear friends and respected colleagues who believe any notion of a "larger plan" or an overarching intelligence is unsubstantiated self-delusion. I have no interest in "converting" them, but I am also at a loss about how to be comforting. If you feel as they do, please understand that I, as author, respect your right to your own ideas.

It seems fair to share my orientation in these matters. In my lifetime, I have shifted from Theosophy to traditional Christian practice to toying with Judaism to acute skepticism to active disbelief. I am now an Animist, which is the most ancient of spiritual systems, preceding paganism or any conceptualization of deities or demons. The ancients knew no separation between themselves and the natural world of plants, animals, weather, and seasonal changes. Differences, yes, in form, function, and apparent consciousness, but not a hierarchical worthiness.

The orchestration of nature (including us) cannot creditably be written off to random chance. No statistician would want to try to give odds on that. *Something* has put it all together. Animism is simple, ancient, and harmonious with the discoveries of modern physics. The animist sees all aspects of creation and the laws that govern them as imbued with spirit, which is neither created nor destroyed. Science says the same thing, but uses the word "energy" instead of spirit.

How these things and laws came into being is incomprehensible. I prefer the construct given by Joseph Campbell, the scholar of mythology and comparative religions. He spoke of "The Transcendent," which was beyond time, duality, and all systems of thought. It is, therefore, outside of our ability to grasp. This satisfies me, and I am left without conflict or the need to further speculate. I suppose this acceptance of what I cannot explain is a leap of faith.

In examining numinous experiences—which, by definition, are life-altering events—and by inviting profound insights, another matter must be addressed: altered consciousness. We operate largely from "ordinary" reality, which is congruent with that of others. That is, we can all agree it is Wednesday, that the weather is damp, and that there are no polar bears in the closet at this time. We deal in the facts, sequences, and analyses with which our very active left brain hemisphere presents us. We read maps, balance checkbooks, and get to the soccer game on time. This mundane reality matters greatly, but it is not the only aspect of consciousness for which we are equipped.

Every child who ever twirled on a swing or adult who "spaced out" watching the windshield wipers on a country road has experienced altered consciousness. Dreaming, feverish delirium, drug tripping, sleep deprivation, alcohol, roller-coaster rides, hormonal changes, hyperventilation, runner's high, orgasm, and pain are but a few of the ways consciousness is altered. Medical hypnosis and biofeedback allow the altering of consciousness so effectively that physical phenomena can be changed (controlling bleeding, painless dentistry, and comfortable childbirth). Mystics in deep contemplation, shamans altered by psychotropic substances, and ordinary people in states of profound emotion also report non-ordinary experiences—altered perceptions of reality. There are creditable "near death" experiences wherein an individual who has apparently died revives and can report what went on around him. Other experiences are of suddenly understanding or "seeing" some important aspects of life previously hidden and feeling compelled to act by the revelation. Lives are changed by such moments. Some of these experiences are inevitable, some dreadful, some enriching. The point is, they exist, and we have all had moments outside of our daily, routine way of perceiving.

My suggestion is to engage whole heartedly in the following ritual, whatever your stance toward the spiritual dimension or altered consciousness.

Ritual Fourteen: Inviting Awareness

Clara, a botanist, belonged to no religious system. When the university she worked for let her go as part of a budget crunch, she lacked a context for dealing with the disruption. At my suggestion, she began to visually observe, both with naked eyes and microscopically, what happens when a cedar tree (her specialty) sustains a wound. She could see that a first response was to seal the injury with protective pitch. On more intimate examination, she found new cells forming immediately to replace those damaged. She drew two immediate conclusions. She needed protection in the short term and that life is ingeniously persistent. Her protection came in the form of conserving her resources and asking for help from colleagues. Healing began when she began to optimistically imagine and pursue a more stable and challenging professional situation.

1. If you have a traditional religious affiliation, spend some time reading about the miracles and transformative events that are reported in your scriptures. Consider and write about how those events could later be seen in relationship to a larger plan.

2. If you are accepting of a spiritual dimension but are not part of any religious system, then consider and write what persuades you that there is more than the physical world in existence. Feelings as well as facts are fully legitimate in this work.

3. If you are not a believer in a spiritual aspect from which would flow numinous experiences, get on the Internet and look up the Hubble Space Telescope pictures. When we look at the astoundingly beautiful pictures of the cosmos sent by the Hubble, it is natural to ask if we are witnessing the creation of form from nothingness—chaos—or a random pattern that may, with study, come to have meaning. The philosophical-religious-mythic implications engage our thought and touch us with wonder. Of course we cannot definitively answer the questions arising: we are looking directly at mystery. And, with mystery, we are faced with questions of our origins with which each of us must individually struggle.

   As you look at the pictures, see if questions come to you about origin, power, infinity, interconnection, or other aspects of creation. Examine your reasoning as to the difference between *chaos* (which is total disorganization from which creativity emerges) and *randomness* (which is unpredictability and is the duality of order). Let questions emerge.

4. Whatever your orientation, look back on your own life to discern a pattern of life-changing events/insights. Consider how your response shaped your later experiences. Does it seem inevitable that you are who you are and where you are? If not, how do you account for your development? Write about this in your journal.

5. Have you ever had a sudden insight or realization that changed your perspective? Have you ever "just known" something out of the ordinary was going to happen? Have you had any experiences remotely like Sylvia's on her vision quest? Take time to write about these things, with a sense of invitation to other spiritually deepening experiences.

CHAPTER 4

Loss of Connection: The Source of Sorrow

There is no wisdom in . . . hopeless sorrow.

—Samuel Johnson

Suffering is the loss of connection. It is alienation from hope, support, pleasure, and source. All suffering is lonely, even when felt in the company of others who are also sorrowful. In a room of people with broken hearts, it is the pain in your own chest that you feel, even though you may empathize with others. No one can "feel what you feel," however kindly their intent. We feel in response to others only as filtered through our own senses and sensibilities, interpreted by our personal experience. We may resonate, care about, and empathize, but do not truly feel the feelings of even our most intimate companions. This loneliness may cripple or it may inspire to productive introspection. It is always our choice.

"There is no wisdom . . . in hopeless sorrow" because wisdom is the distillation of experience and experience gives reason to be hopeful. When you forget this, your alienation is not only from the person, place, condition, or object lost to you, but from your own life experience.

Separation from Self

Most people define themselves in terms of action roles and relationships. If you are a doctor, you probably think in terms of treatments, colleagues, and patients. If you are a mother, most likely you think of yourself in relationship to the pains and pleasures of parenthood as well as intimacy with your children. If you are a salesperson, then it is customers, managers, and quotas that will occupy your mind. Teachers think of students and subject matter, just as a farmer will be involved with crops, land, and markets. In all these roles and relationships, the focus is outward. This looking outward is necessary to live in the world, but it's not the whole picture.

You must have an intimacy with yourself *separate from other relationships*. It is critical to how you navigate in the world and in your life. If you haven't taken time or energy to define or get well-acquainted with your "self," when sorrow comes, you are missing *the* critical resource to heal and grow. *Self*, in this usage, is the amalgam of body, mind, emotions, and spirit.

Body

It is a sad truth that in this appearance-obsessed culture, your relationship with your body may be largely critical. Your primary conscious interaction with your body may be thinking it's not muscular enough, too skinny or fat, or any of thousands of unkind comparisons to some fancied ideal. You may rail at a body part that is functioning poorly and giving pain, denying yourself compassion or the nurturing challenge to heal. Unfortunately, you may be inattentive to your body except when in pain or sexually stimulated. A frightening majority of modern people give less thoughtful care, maintenance, and affection to their hardworking bodies than they would to a beast of burden or a machine. This alienation serves them poorly in times of sorrow and, in reality, contributes to their suffering. This lack of intimacy with our bodies is pervasive and incredibly wasteful and hurtful.

The following ritual is designed to stimulate your thinking and experience of the wondrous temple you occupy and inspire the same appreciation for it that you'd feel for any intricate work of art. You live in your body. It is home. It is the tool of living, and through your senses, you have learned all that you now know.

Ritual Fifteen: Finding Your Body

Jackie was dangerously obese and so self-condemning about it that she was unable to let more than a few minutes pass without calling herself demeaning names—"Fatty," "Porky," "blimp," and so on. She brought in a picture of herself twenty years before as a foxy cheerleader. She'd begun to pile on the weight after the birth of her third child, a girl with Down's syndrome. The last thing she wanted was to be in touch with her body, as she'd hidden her deep sorrow under layers of fat. Performing ritual below was one step in regaining contact with the still-functioning parts of her physical being and encouraging her to be much more compassionate. These were necessary steps for Jackie to change.

1. Remember to perform your four-stroke breathing ritual.

2. Using the list below, rate your relationship with your physical being. The higher the number, the more you agree with the statement.

Example: My body is worthy of appreciation.

1	**x**	3		5
Not at all				fully

On this example, the score is 2.

I like the looks of my:

____ face

1	3	5
Not at all		fully

____ skin

1	3	5
Not at all		fully

____ hair

1	3	5
Not at all		fully

____ eyes

1	3	5
Not at all		fully

____ mouth

1	3	5
Not at all		fully

____ nose

1	3	5
Not at all		fully

____ teeth

1	3	5
Not at all		fully

____ neck

1	3	5
Not at all		fully

____ shoulders

1	3	5
Not at all		fully

____ arms

1	3	5
Not at all		fully

____ hands

1	3	5
Not at all		fully

____ upper back

1	3	5
Not at all		fully

____ lower back

1	3	5
Not at all		fully

____ chest

1	3	5
Not at all		fully

____ abdomen

1	3	5
Not at all		fully

____ genitals

1	3	5
Not at all		fully

____ thighs

1	3	5
Not at all		fully

____ knees

1	3	5
Not at all		fully

____ calves   1_____3_____5
                   Not at all   fully

____ ankles   1_____3_____5
                   Not at all   fully

____ feet   1_____3_____5
                   Not at all   fully

I approve of the functioning of my:

____ digestive tract   1_____3_____5
                        Not at all   fully

____ skin   1_____3_____5
                   Not at all   fully

____ heart   1_____3_____5
                   Not at all   fully

____ eyes   1_____3_____5
                   Not at all   fully

____ lungs   1_____3_____5
                   Not at all   fully

____ nose   1_____3_____5
                   Not at all   fully

____ teeth   1_____3_____5
                   Not at all   fully

____ neck   1_____3_____5
                   Not at all   fully

____ shoulders   1_____3_____5
                   Not at all   fully

____ arms   1_____3_____5
                   Not at all   fully

____ hands   1_____3_____5
                   Not at all   fully

____ upper back   1_____3_____5
                   Not at all   fully

____ lower back   1_____3_____5
                   Not at all   fully

____ endocrine system 1_____3_____5
                      Not at all   fully

____ digestive system   1_____3_____5
                     Not at all   fully

____ genitals   1_____3_____5
                     Not at all   fully

____ reproductive system 1_____3_____5
                     Not at all   fully

____ immune system   1_____3_____5
                     Not at all   fully

____ legs   1_____3_____5
                     Not at all   fully

____ nervous system   1_____3_____5
                     Not at all   fully

____ ears   1_____3_____5
                     Not at all   fully

____ circulatory system   1_____3_____5
                     Not at all   fully

____ feet   1_____3_____5
                     Not at all   fully

____ I am attentive to my body's messages of fatigue.
    1_____3_____5
Not at all   fully

____ I am attentive to my body's messages of pain or discomfort.
    1_____3_____5
Not at all   fully

____ I am as kind to my body as I am to the bodies of those I love.
    1_____3_____5
Not at all   fully

____ I provide my body with good nutrition.
    1_____3_____5
Not at all   fully

____ I eat in a pleasant atmosphere.
    1_____3_____5
Not at all   fully

____ I consult health-care professionals regularly, both for prevention of problems
    and for treatment of ills.
    1_____3_____5
Not at all   fully

____ I rest midday when I am tired or drowsy.

1 _____ 3 _____ 5
Not at all   fully

____ I get sufficient sleep.

1 _____ 3 _____ 5
Not at all   fully

____ I am aware of and honor my biorhythms.

1 _____ 3 _____ 5
Not at all   fully

____ I exercise regularly and appropriately for my body's capability.

1 _____ 3 _____ 5
Not at all   fully

____ I moderate my indulgences in rich food, alcohol, or drugs.

1 _____ 3 _____ 5
Not at all   fully

____ I treat my body to regular massages or other pleasant, nondemanding experiences.

1 _____ 3 _____ 5
Not at all   fully

____ I am thoughtful about the physical tasks or challenges I ask my body to perform.

1 _____ 3 _____ 5
Not at all   fully

____ I adorn and/or otherwise enhance my body's appearance.

1 _____ 3 _____ 5
Not at all   fully

____ I am peaceful with the marks of living on my body.

1 _____ 3 _____ 5
Not at all   fully

____ I am appreciative of all the service my body has performed silently for me.

1 _____ 3 _____ 5
Not at all   fully

____ I treat my body as a good friend.

1 _____ 3 _____ 5
Not at all   fully

3. Now add up your score for this whole section. A score of around 250 is marvelous! Congratulations on the friendship you have with your physical being. A score of around 180 is pretty good. You've a starting point for fully living in and appreciating the gift that is your body. A score less than 150 is a sign that not all is well with this important relationship.

4. See which section (appearance or function) needs attention. Maybe both!

5. With this information in front of you, begin to formulate a plan for a compassionate, supportive, enjoyable friendship with your body.

Mind

"I think, therefore I am" was the statement of Rene Descartes, the French philosopher. He was discussing the mysterious idea of consciousness. Certainly thinking defines an enormous part of human identity. Mechanical, abstract, and creative intelligence, as well as memory, are components. The capacity to be aware of ourselves *as we act* is a function of mind. We are both the "eye in the sky" and the phenomenon observed—a most complex idea.

It was of some use, but overrated, when intelligence quotients (IQs) were devised early in the last century. A problem arose from the name. "Intelligence" is more than the prediction of academic success, which is what IQ tests are largely useful in doing. Intelligence is popularly, but inadequately, defined in terms of left hemisphere brain functions: problem-solving, computation, verbal skills, persistence, memory, abstraction, and application.

In our lopsided society, the popular successes are those folks who are clever with money-making, creating ingenious devices (and getting them to market), or entertaining in one way or another. Rewards, generally money or acclaim, come for "having a good head on your shoulders," being a "smart cookie," or "smart as a whip." The ability to operate analytically, which involves goal-directedness, time-awareness, language, sequences, and logic, is highly valued and is called "linear thinking." These functions are performed by the left hemisphere of the brain. You may make the mistake of calling yourself names if this isn't your long suit. That is wasteful of energy better spent finding an appreciation of what you do well and opening yourself to development in the areas where you feel disadvantaged. We are anatomically and psychically called to find balance.

Balance would suggest that nonlinear mind processes and products are equally valuable. These things spring from the brain's intuitive, spatial, sensory, feeling, creative right hemisphere, which has no relationship to time.

It is common to meet people profoundly out of balance in these dimensions. You already know if you'd rather solve a mechanical problem or write a poem, but doing the following ritual will help you see where your strength lies. If you feel seriously "out of whack," spend more time cultivating the rest of your intelligence, the side you use less often. After all, a whole brain is better than half a brain.

Ritual Sixteen: Rediscovering Your Mind

1. Begin with ritual 1.

2. Using the scale you've become familiar with in earlier rituals, score how well you agree with the statements.

Group One

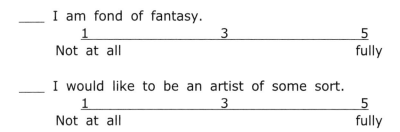

____ I am fond of fantasy.

1	3	5
Not at all		fully

____ I would like to be an artist of some sort.

1	3	5
Not at all		fully

____ I like music, drawing, and/or crafts, which interest me greatly.

1_____3_____5

Not at all   fully

____ I am normally a playful person.

1_____3_____5

Not at all   fully

____ I typically react emotionally.

1_____3_____5

Not at all   fully

____ I am empathetic.

1_____3_____5

Not at all   fully

____ I lose track of time easily.

1_____3_____5

Not at all   fully

____ I have creative impulses.

1_____3_____5

Not at all   fully

____ Jigsaw puzzles are fun.

1_____3_____5

Not at all   fully

____ I am naturally impulsive and spontaneous.

1_____3_____5

Not at all   fully

Total score for this section: _____

Group Two

____ I am logical.

1_____3_____5

Not at all   fully

____ I have a good grasp of time management.

1_____3_____5

Not at all   fully

____ I am orderly.

1_____3_____5

Not at all   fully

____ I am able to analyze the elements of a problem.

1_____3_____5

Not at all   fully

____ I seldom get rattled.

1   3   5

Not at all   fully

____ I prefer to think rather than react.

1   3   5

Not at all   fully

____ I am systematic.

1   3   5

Not at all   fully

____ I like predictability.

1   3   5

Not at all   fully

____ I am able to follow through on long projects.

1   3   5

Not at all   fully

____ My reading is largely technical.

1   3   5

Not at all   fully

Total score for this section: _____

Group One, of course, gives indications of your level of right hemisphere affinity and Group Two of the left side. This ritual will encourage you to think more about the *how* you think, and the *what* of your intelligence. It feels good to operate in your most familiar mode, but equally satisfying to venture into the other hemisphere's arena and add to your repertoire.

Separation from Others

It is well established and easily observable that people vary in their desire for relationships. Those known as extroverts are outgoing and eager to be with others, while introverts tend to keep to themselves and be less socially visible. Almost no one, of course, is all or nothing because the needs for human contact and companionship as well as "alone time" are built into our psyches. The degree and mode of relating is individual. An introvert may have no more than one or two intimate companions and see them infrequently, but may see these relationships as precious resources not to be wasted. The extrovert will probably have many acquaintances and a few good friends or close family members. It is important for her to maintain contact with people in times of grief because it helps to maintain a familiar routine, and because they are a source of comfort.

Serious trouble may be brewing when a person withdraws or isolates themselves for *extended periods*, rebuffing overtures of loving concern. When a person is suffering, it is natural for them to pull away from superficial activities and "go deeper" into the important issues of loss and life. However, if you cut off the support of empathic friends and family, you will amplify your sense of loss, making recovery more difficult.

As always, the wholesome, life-supportive path is between the extremes of alienated in-turning and frantic outreach. If, for some reason, you have no one to turn to, as a therapist, I urge you to seek counseling, go to a grief support group (check your local hospital), or engage in some quiet activity that brings you into the company of others. This may feel strange or frightening, but some contact is a key element in finding meaning in life after a loss.

The next ritual is brief and will reinforce that it is natural and fine to be in either mode. It will also encourage you to allow the solace of human companionship to soften your suffering.

Ritual Seventeen: Introvert or Extrovert?

1. For the good of your body, mind, and emotions, do your four-stroke breathing ritual.

2. You know the routine by now: this ritual will confirm what you know about your own nature.

Group One

____ I am ordinarily fond of being with people.

1	3	5
Not at all		fully

____ I like to be in the middle of activities, to know what's happening.

1	3	5
Not at all		fully

____ I usually like planning birthday parties and other gala events.

1	3	5
Not at all		fully

____ I am normally a playful person.

1	3	5
Not at all		fully

____ I typically reach out to get acquainted when someone new shows up at work.

1	3	5
Not at all		fully

____ I am a soft touch for a sad story.

1	3	5
Not at all		fully

____ I am just fine with standing up in a group and having my say.

1	3	5
Not at all		fully

____ I have a lot of friends.

1	3	5
Not at all		fully

____ I usually take other people's disapproval to heart.

1_____3_____5
Not at all   fully

____ I naturally look to others for validation.

1_____3_____5
Not at all   fully

Total score for this section: _____

Group Two

____ I prefer being alone to being in a crowd.

1_____3_____5
Not at all   fully

____ I have a few friends that I have known for years.

1_____3_____5
Not at all   fully

____ I rarely or never confide in others.

1_____3_____5
Not at all   fully

____ Traveling alone is my preference.

1_____3_____5
Not at all   fully

____ I am likely to avoid a social event.

1_____3_____5
Not at all   fully

____ My life is one of internal dialogue rather than outward discourse.

1_____3_____5
Not at all   fully

____ I fear being "taken over" if I allow people to get too close.

1_____3_____5
Not at all   fully

____ My life revolves around ideas or projects rather than people.

1_____3_____5
Not at all   fully

____ I like to give gifts anonymously.

1_____3_____5
Not at all   fully

____ I am uneasy when attention is drawn to me.

1_____3_____5
Not at all   fully

Total score for this section: _____

3. As you've surmised, Group One partially defines the extroverted personality and Group Two, the introverted. While it is proper to honor your own innate nature, extremes of either form will inhibit healing from loss.

Separation from the Familiar

"You can't go home again," "You never step in the same river twice," and "Yesterday is dead and gone" are familiar phrases indicating perpetual change. We become accustomed to places, routines, things, times of life, and predictability. There is a comforting illusion of stability in these things, hence separation from the familiar is often a painful and surprising loss.

Finding what is satisfying and hopeful in the present moment is good advice that's easy to say and often hard to do. When you have happy memories and comforting associations, you will feel an aching nostalgia for what is past. If you believed yourself dependent on a setting or conditions now unavailable to you, there will be fear and even resentment.

Some changes occur through the passage of time: the slim young girl becomes the full-bodied woman, who becomes the frail old granny. Until there is acceptance of this inevitability as evidence of individuation, each change will be felt as loss.

To be displaced from a homeland or place where you've known fulfillment is disorienting. The question arises, "Who am I, now that I live far from the ocean?"

The loss of the familiar is particularly grievous when it is unanticipated and, hence, startling. It seems necessary to grieve for *what was* in order to embrace *what is* and get on with life. Some part of that process is acknowledging the importance of the familiar in shaping us. That is what part of this book is about.

Ritual Eighteen: Thanking the Familiar

You are familiar with how to begin this ritual.

Write a few paragraphs on each of the following things. In your writing, specifically note the importance you attach to each one and *clearly give it thanks for existing in your life.*

a. A place
   Example: I remember the house on Pio Pico Street where I was born . . . (two paragraphs later) I am grateful that I had that stability for all those years.

b. An object
   Example: When the petty thief took my grandmother's watch off its display, I remembered. . . .

c. A time of life
   Example: When I was a young mother and my children were still with me, I used to bake bread in the early afternoon so the house would smell good when they got home from school. . . .

d. A role
   Example: Being chosen to teach honors English was. . . .

e. A condition
   Example: Once I was a strong enough swimmer to compete in ocean racing. . . .

Separation from Illusions

Illusions are effects or ideas that give the appearance of truth but are actually false. Magicians, politicians, statisticians, advertisers, and our own personal myths present us with an endless parade of illusions, some pleasant, some seductive, some vicious; all of them distracting us from truth. The loss of a cherished illusion is painful.

You must not make the mistake that in abandoning illusion you are abandoning hope. *Hope is an attitude, a mind-set, a way of choosing a direction.* Hope is a broad, general way of looking at life. It is fundamental to healing and growth. Illusion is specific and not testable. The test of hope is that we have all survived and many of us thrive.

There are four main types of illusion and two subcategories. First, *I can do anything*. This is the illusion of ultimate control, which often comes from the curse of perfectionism. Perfectionism extracts intense, exhausting effort that inevitably comes up short, thereby dooming the victim to a sense of continual inadequacy. You, who are still learning and exploring life, are in *process*, therefore unperfected. How absurd to act as if your *products* should be more finished than you are.

This is not an apology for shoddy work, rather a plea for the view that every effort is a rung upward on the learning ladder. As you gain experience, your craft and your life will be refined. Not perfected—refined. Good, responsible effort applied humanely is the idea. Therein lies satisfaction, not in driven unrest.

Another manifestation of the *I can do anything* illusion is that of power over circumstances that are not given to you to control or manage. The idea that *if I am just good (loving, helpful, instructive) enough, the person I care about will be healed (shown, protected, improved)* is illusory. Change doesn't happen that way.

Parents often fall into this conceit, as if they were the sole force acting on their children. True, they are undeniably vital influences, teaching by what they do and don't do, say and don't say—but they are only part of the mosaic. The intent to control another person, whether partner, colleague, or child, is almost always doomed to fail or, if successful, to cripple. Part of free will, let alone karma, is that you have choice and unique circumstances. It is the individual person who must ultimately choose. To believe differently is to play puppet or puppet master.

Often personal ambitions fall into the *I can do anything* illusory realm in the *if only* subcategory. If, as a child, you wanted and expected to be a prima ballerina or a reincarnated Mick Jagger, that was a dream to work toward with lessons, practice, and dedication. It's fine and good to believe in yourself. No need, at that point, to talk of the odds against success or the luck required for the dream to become real.

However, when life intervened with the need to earn your daily bread, find a partner, and enter adult life, your dedication to the dream and to the work required for it to have any possibility of fulfillment almost certainly was compromised. You chose to direct your energies otherwise in a more traditional, achievable way for a very good reason: you wanted to do so.

Holding to the illusion of likely stardom in a demanding, unforgiving theater world becomes torment and a cause of unrest. It is a loss of reality. The dream could segue into an illusion that stardom could have been yours, *if only* you hadn't chosen such an ordinary life, or *if only* you hadn't had kids or, worse, *if only* all the cards hadn't been stacked against you.

The *if only* illusion is dangerous because it will hold you back from actual satisfactions. There is no reason you can't take dance or music classes now to refresh your talent, perform locally, and experience the heady pleasure of applause. This is possible. To become a Maria

Tallchief look-alike or a glittering international rock star is not at all probable. Such truth is painful to realize and brings sadness. It is a loss of illusion.

The second subset of the *I can do anything* illusion is the one that says *the rules don't apply to me*. There is sort of invincibility to this one. It leads to believing that, because you are healthy and have a good genetic inheritance, you can eat any sort of food, drink endless quaffs of alcohol, take any legal or illegal drug in quantity, and forget exercise. It is the illusion that says, because you are lively and young of heart, you can marry a twenty-year-old when you are sixty without there being a price. *The rules don't apply to me* illusion would have you characteristically and without research or reflection gambling against the odds. It is the ultimate loser's game. While it is suffocating to color only within the lines, never take a risk, and be sheepishly compliant to your local social standards, the illusion of being outside the forces shaping human experience is the stuff of suffering.

The second major category of illusion is *I can do nothing*. This throwing up of hands results from the loss of hope, which is known as despair. Those who are acutely aware of the assault on the living body of Earth, the food supply, and essential liberties are in deadly danger of having hope extinguished.

Nihilism is the philosophy denying that there is any objective standard for truth. Moral nihilism denies any objective validity in ethical suppositions. It is the "Eat, drink, and be merry, for tomorrow we die" philosophy that abandons thought and community. A more subtle, wholesome, realistic philosophy says, "It is today we live." If you are to engage with life responsibly, you must stop skating and begin swimming.

The nihilism of the *I can do nothing* illusion in relationships and neighborhoods leads to coarse self-serving. To buy into the absurdity of *I can do nothing* is to deny your talents, interests, and power. Whether you are talking about an ecosystem, a family, or a political equation it is manifestly clear that you *can* do something. How effective you are is both another question and a measure of who joins you in the effort. Intention to put energy into what you love counts.

Illusion three is *every story is about me*. In examining many lives, I'm struck with how easily we fall into the notion that we are causal in all the suffering of others or, conversely, that everything is directed at us personally and we are only wounded victims.

I counseled a man whose wife had died of breast cancer. He believed that if he'd been more alert the lump would have been discovered early and she would have been saved. Her death became his responsibility; the story was about him.

Classic is the parent who wails at the wayward child, "Why have you done this to me?" It doesn't matters if the kid is pregnant, arrested for driving drunk, or has failed in long division; the parent makes the story his own. In so doing, the power and/or responsibility for foolishness becomes the adult's story. What's the message? One of two: 1) I have no responsibility because my parent should have controlled me, or 2) Now I know how to punish my parents through my irresponsibility.

If you believe that what you sow is what you reap and that what goes around comes around (karma), then it follows that what others choose isn't all about you. You may be affected, certainly. However, you are at best a supporting player and not the whole hoo-ha—no matter how much you care. Accepting and respecting that others dear to us have their own dramas saves endless interfering frustration. Reality testing is a good thing. You can begin by working on the following ritual.

Ritual Nineteen: Facing Illusions

It is a major challenge to face the illusions that haunt you and keep you stuck in unproductive thought patterns, but until you do, your energy will often simply churn impotently. When that energy is freed, you may direct it however you choose.

1. Write a few paragraphs on the theme of *I can do anything*, then examine these assumptions from the realistic part of your mind. Do they seem accurate and possible? If you decide to give them up, write more about your intentions for the energy you will release.

   Example of a beginning: *I can keep a perfect house, go to all my kids' games, be an alluring sexual partner, take care of my aging parents, and hold down an executive job without raising a sweat.*

2. Write a few paragraphs on the theme of *if only*, then examine these assumptions from the realistic part of your mind and write more about your intentions for the energy you will release.

   Example of a beginning: *If only Debby hadn't gotten pregnant, I'd be head of medical services at Cedars of Lebanon Hospital. . . .*

3. Write a few paragraphs on the theme of *the rules don't apply to me*, then examine these assumptions from the realistic part of your mind and write more about your intentions for the energy you will release.

   Example of a beginning: *I can live healthily on anything, even bean dip, Ding Dongs, and thrice-boiled coffee.*

4. Write a few paragraphs on the theme of *I can do nothing*, then examine these assumptions from the realistic part of your mind and write more about your intentions for the energy you will release.

   Example of a beginning: *Nothing I do really matters, whether it's recycling, taking the kids to the park, or trying to figure out my taxes.*

5. Write a few paragraphs on the theme of *every story is about me*, then examine these assumptions from the realistic part of your mind and write more about your intentions for the energy you will release.

   Example of a beginning: *It's all my fault that Jackie wasn't chosen prom queen. If I'd made her a better dress. . . .*

Separation from the Sacred

Spiritual awakening, as used in this book, *is coming into awareness of empowerment and direction beyond that of ordinary consciousness.* If you have a core acceptance that you are not a random event in the universe, but are the product of a transcendent intention (however you conceptualize the source of that intention), then you can begin to perceive some order to the chaotic events that have resulted in your current sorrow. Lacking a sense of connection or participation in the divine is terribly lonely.

The rational mind is supremely useful in ordering daily life, in problem-solving, and in speculative musings. Without its ability to plan, analyze, and process factual information, many of the advances that distinguish us from other species could not have occurred. But rational abilities do not account for the capacity for rapture, nor can they sustain us in the throes of profound loss.

When you grieve, you may find yourselves asking "Why? Why him? Why not me?" You are compelled to find answers to give meaning to your loss. Coming to view your life and what is lost to you as part of a larger plan is humankind's venerable solution for bringing order to the emotional chaos of terrible bereavement.

An axiom, often heard during World War II, is that *"there are no atheists in foxholes."* The primal awareness of impending death elicits pleas for assistance from beyond and confronts you with the need to make meaning of your life. For uncounted generations, humankind has derived that meaning in terms of a divine or overarching intelligence that directs destiny. Humankind resists notions of randomness about life and death. In our vulnerability, we seek ways to find meaning and purpose about inevitabilities we cannot control.

Modern people are no different than their ancestors in needing guiding myths to provide frameworks for leading purposeful lives. Myths are not simply comforting (or terrifying) stories; they are the result and expression of deep, often wordless experience. A numinous moment is one that physically-psychically connects you with parts of yourself ordinarily hidden. You may experience blinding insight, firm inner instruction, or a "knowingness" that surpasses any previous convictions. When you have had such an opening of consciousness, you are forever changed. This sort of awakening brings you to an unassailable understanding that there is reason and purpose in your existence. How this purpose is revealed, how you describe its origins and power, and how sturdily you live your intentions is an individual matter.

Ritual Twenty: Inviting the Sacred

This is a time to really focus on ritual 1. It is of tremendous help in moving into a deeper, quieter, more intuitive consciousness.

In order to invite the intuitive wisdom that is waiting to be recognized, it is necessary to stop the hurry-hurry, circular questioning, and endless commentary of the busy, rational, analytic, left brain hemisphere. Whether you call it prayer, meditation, contemplation, spacing out, or resting, set aside at least half an hour daily for a week. Early morning, before the hassles of daily life come thundering in to disturb your quiet, is very good.

1. Sit comfortably.

2. Do your four-stroke breathing with the following pattern:
   empty yourself of confusion, be empty, fill yourself with trust,
   be full of trust. Do this repeatedly at a pace that feels natural to you.

3. Look intently, without criticism or analysis, at something intricate and beautiful: a shell, stone, flower, candle flame, or a landscape.

4. Occupy your busy mind and calm your restlessness with one of the following:

   a. Humming like a bee in clover

   b. Chanting a series of words like "peace-calm-truth" or "love-healing-kindness" or "understanding-purpose-unity." Feel free to choose your own litany.

    c. Following the movement of the candle flame's smoke or something else, like clouds or the surface of moving water

    d. Following the passage of air through your nose, to your lungs, and out your mouth in peaceful, unhurried movement

In this way, you invite the sacred, which often first shows itself as intuitive knowing.

The Essential Separation: Goodbye

To say "goodbye" is to invite release. It is a breaking of energetic ties, an acceptance that a connection is ending. This is a profoundly difficult part of the sorrow and grief process. It is as essential as breath if you are to move beyond sorrow into pleasure.

When we resist—and almost everyone does—the need to face the reality that a person, place, time of life, or perspective has forever changed, we are in danger of letting our sorrow become an inalterable condition. To say "goodbye" is not to have amnesia nor forget what has mattered. It is not disloyalty nor demonstration that the person or situation is a throw-away. It means breaking the emotional and energetic bond. What was vivid fades, rather like an old photograph. The freed energy is then available for adaptation and expanded possibilities.

I am providing this insight to prepare you for the work ahead. It is a culminating part of the process, one for which you will be ready at the end of the next section, "Tools for Alchemical Transformation." I suggest you reward yourself with a special meal, an outing, or other treat for having come so far in this difficult and necessary work.

PART II

Tools for Alchemical Transformation

CHAPTER 5

Seeing How to Move Forward

Forward, forward let us range,
Let the great world spin ever down the ringing grooves of change.

—Tennyson

For many people, transformation as a dynamic self-directed process is a difficult concept. Simply put, to direct the inevitable changes in your perspective and experience requires three things. First must come the recognition that change is not only desirable, but possible. This implies hope, if not belief. Second must come determination to marshal all possible resources—friends, therapy, experience, tools—to the task. Further, you must adopt an attitude of humane expectation toward your efforts. That means if sometimes you do things poorly or forget, you do not bitterly chastise yourself, but pull up your socks and begin again with a kind and honest assessment of your efforts. Finally, you will need to consistently practice what you've learned before it can become integrated into your life. Those looking for quick fixes will be disappointed. Those willing to reorder their thinking and behavior will benefit. It really is that simple and that challenging.

My intent in this final section of the book is to show some ways that people—including myself—have learned to transmute the anguish of loss into wholesome, creative living. I also want to provide a set of techniques and personal rituals by which you may find such a path within yourself. I refer to this process as "expressive grief work."

I know something about this process from several vantage points. I am a psychotherapist, a widow who has remarried, and the parent of both living and dead adult children. As a therapist working with emotionally wounded people during much of my career, I have had an intimate involvement with human despair. Several clients chose to die; many more threatened to do so. Much of the human pain I have seen has been that of people learning to transcend loss and separation from essential parts of their lives. Many have learned to disarm their discouragement and invoke hope. I have profound respect for their strength and courage to undergo this transformation into vital living.

My credentials for writing this section were also hard earned in my personal life through the excruciating lessons that grew out of my husband Joe's suicide and, four years later, that of my son Patrick. In my long life I have lost place, status, illusion, direction, and companionship. I have had an intimate relationship with sorrow. While I certainly do not present myself as a paragon, I have been refined and deepened by my encounters with these things. I have learned enough to be confident that I grasp the principles of alchemical transformation. Remember, always, that hope is the philosopher's stone catalyzing common sorrow into the gold of creative living. As I write, I am happy. It is my profound hope that you will have the stamina and hope to do your own expressive grief work, emerging with pleasure permeating your life as it does mine.

I have had to learn a great deal about how to face sorrow, and I have a good deal of trepidation about holding out my experiences as a model. What was useful for me may or may not be useful for you. Each of us must come to terms with grief in our unique way, so I invite you to take what may be of value from my experiences and to discard what is not. I also feel reluctant to expose my own warts and vulgarity, but dealing with grief is a great equalizer. To pretend that I have some kind of "professional immunity" to base responses and to present only my finer insights and moments of emotional reconciliation would neither ring true nor fairly portray the process.

In 1732 Thomas Fuller wrote that "No man should be afraid to die, who hath understood what it is to live." When we believe death to be inappropriate and unfair, the pain of bereavement is particularly harsh. The death of a dewy bride wracks us far more than the death of an exhausted old woman. When my brilliant and creative son, Patrick, died, a particularly bitter pill for me was the loss of the books that would be forever unwritten, the artistic statements that died with him, and the unconceived children he might have fathered. It was the loss of his *potential*—that fragment of my hope—that I was most reluctant to yield to the awful reality of his death. I felt that he had not understood what it was to live, and I could not reconcile his voluntary embracing of death.

When we are bereaved—left alive when someone dear has died—we are sorrowful. When we have lost our place in the world, seen illusions shattered, or experienced other, uninvited change, anger, confusion, denial, terror, and despair may invade our hearts. Our feelings will be powerful, perhaps foreign, and will dominate our existence.

Expressive Grief Work

In the alchemy of transmuting grief and anguish into wisdom and creativity, emotional expression is a central activity. "Psychological discharge," "ventilation," or "catharsis" are terms for describing the core emotional process in conscious, ritualized grieving. In Orthodox Jewish tradition, "sitting shiva" allows seven days for the family and other bereaved during which they are supported, expected, and encouraged to experience and *express* their anguish. All other duties are suspended. Details of living are tended by others. Mirrors are covered to symbolize the need to turn inward; black is worn in mourning; burial is prompt. Weeping, keening, talking, remembering, regretting, appreciating, and *emptying out* feelings are in order. These are basic ingredients in the grief process.

Whether we "sit shiva," sob on our pillows, confide in our spiritual advisors or seek professional psychotherapy, emptying out is part of the growth necessary to transmute grief to creativity and to foster the rebirth of pleasure. To contain, deny, or repress our pain may lead to personality-distorting depression.

There are two main sorts of depression: reactive and chronic. Reactive depression is a natural, transitory response to physical or emotional loss. The body husbands its resources and the mind works desperately to blunt the anguish. Energy is unavailable, feelings are muffled, and helplessness overwhelms the sufferer. Time will, to a degree, heal this sort of depression.

Chronic depression is an insidious stagnation that does not yield easily to time, fresh stimuli, or inspirational talks. It may be genetic and unremitting, or it may begin as a reactive depression and become entrenched. The body "turns off" and distorts natural needs for sleep and food into excesses or denials. Hopelessness is the pervasive experience of the chronically depressed. A meaningless, featureless apathy distorts life. The juice is gone. Death is attractive, but we are afraid and condemn ourselves as cowards.

A semblance of normality is maintained by sticking to ordinary routines—get up, go to work, be polite, shop for food, fix supper, go to bed. But repressed misery will leak into our thoughts, actions, and emotions. Tears may start unexpectedly, as they did once for me, when I saw a tall, red-blond man sitting pensively on a park bench. The quick impression resurrected Patrick's image before me. With the vision came the realization that I would never, ever again sit with him under a eucalyptus tree and watch the sunset, commenting on the charming accent of Russian countesses.

Strange fears may grow in us when we are heavy with grief. Danger seems all around. Nowhere are we safe. Dread anticipation poisons the mind and body. Sleep may be elusive, and bad dreams may haunt the hours that should be bringing rest and renewal.

"After all," I reasoned, "if it could happen to Patrick, it could happen to Katie, Stan, or Peter," my younger, surviving children. The pleasure and comfort I might have taken from them was burned away, leaving ashes. Terror at the thought—even the expectation—of their deaths distorted my love to a smothering kind of protectiveness that interfered with our relationships. Fear became my companion. I was comfortless: "un-comfort-able." I was acutely aware of my own mortality, the tick of the clock, the turning of calendar pages. These are some of the painful qualities of sorrow.

New commitments may feel too dangerous. Bottled up, we see death as a treachery, a violation of an unwritten contract with God or with the dead person. The contract, unspoken and unacknowledged until it was broken, stated that either we were to be permitted to die first or that death would come in old age as a welcome release. How can we commit to anything after such a betrayal?

Unexpressed, this anger is a hot coal scorching our capacity to express love. Resentful suspicions about the meaning of life and the motives of God turn us bitter. We isolate ourselves. Sometimes we even think that "no one understands."

It is clear that body and mind interact intimately. Many a peptic ulcer has been traced to an agitated mind. Containing grief carries a fearful danger of physical and emotional sickness. We do, literally, have wounds from our sufferings—the broken heart you feel in your chest is the real, beating organ that pumps your blood. Unrelieved sorrow has led many to seek solace in alcohol and drugs or to retreat to the living death of mental withdrawal.

We may feel guilty for being alive, or we may obsess on our failings—fancied and real—to our dead companion or other sorrowful loss. Guilt is an acid etching and obliterating our self-respect, hope, and good memories. It works its brutality on our souls and may demoralize us so fully that we forget our virtues, our sacrifices, our successes, our love.

Unexorcised, guilt is a foul, debilitating presence in our lives, turning us away from all that is wholesome and healing.

It is not necessary to live with guilt. Guilt can be exorcised, restitution made, absolution self-granted. For some of us, it takes a strong expressive effort to do so. We may need outside help.

I have experienced the alchemical fire of grief many times in my life. I am not unusual in this. After having listened to literally hundreds of people dealing with their lives—their confusion, grief, outrage, inadequacy, love, and spirituality—I *know* that we are all given repeated opportunities to refine ourselves. I believe that the failure to learn and grow from these tests is the supreme tragedy of life. Not to do so is to risk—even invite—physical and emotional disability.

In one four-year period, my stamina and courage were tested severely. My beloved father had an accident with his radial-arm saw, leaving four fingers on the bench. Three months later, he died of emphysema and a stroke. My husband killed himself with a large bore rifle in our bedroom. At the time, my four children were in the throes of adolescence and I lost my job. It looked as if I was going to lose the home my father and grandfather had built and in which I had been born. Then, four years later, my brilliant, charming, depressive son suicided. Through it all, I appeared to function reasonably well, with time out for private despair—but my body couldn't be deceived. My physical movements reflected my bitter grief and eroding courage. I fell apart and had to stay in bed for three months, my back nearly destroyed. I'd gamely "referred" my tension to my spine.

I believe that the primary reason I've become a thriving survivor is due to my incredible good fortune in having a circle of wise friends, skilled in the healing arts, who challenged me to live. The existence of my other children was, of course, also a powerful motivation. Later, I'll discuss various personal rituals for healing that I have either used myself or have seen used with great effectiveness.

In the pained confusion of our bereavement, we may fear that we will be disloyal if we express our grief, transcend the moment, and go on with our lives. Somewhat absurdly, we fear that we will forget. I remember well the first time after Patrick's death that I had a liberating belly laugh at some silly movie; the world stopped in a frozen frame of time. I heard my voice laughing, felt the release in my chest, and knew that I had forgotten for a few moments.

Questions flooded in. Was I disloyal? A negligent mother? Had I forgotten? Was I wrong to be amused by the pratfalls on the screen? For me, the answer was "No!" Not when I remembered the laughs Patrick and I shared, his wicked sense of humor, and his pleasure in goofiness. Enjoyment was part of him and part of me. Fun was a bond that held us close. Far from "forgetting" him, I was able, at long last, to smile when I thought of my son.

As we express our guilt, anger, loneliness, and fear appropriately, we become less obsessed, less compulsive, less haunted by miserable images and unhappy conjecture. The refining fire of grief can clear much room for laughter, creativity, affection, and curiosity. I find that my stamina and compassion have grown, and most importantly, I believe there is purpose in my life and in all life. And there is a community of survivors who have come to the same conclusion.

The word "appropriately" in the last paragraph has special importance. First, appropriate grief work furthers the grieving process. It *accomplishes* something—ventilation, providing insight, planning. It is not a fruitless, endlessly chanted mantra of misery. Second, appropriate grief work doesn't exploit others. Comforters may feel empathic pain, but the mourner is not parasitically feeding off their energy. Rather, the mourner is eliciting understanding and sharing. The transactions are clean and the caring is received with recognition that it is not a substitute for remaining actively involved in furthering one's inner work.

When our energy becomes stagnant, we may try to revive it by reaching out to others. It is one thing to lament and keen while sitting shiva or grieving in the arms of a friend when pain is tearing our hearts and guts. To allow a friend to provide genuine comfort is to give a great privilege. But it is quite another thing to wring pity and concessions from our companions by drearily displaying our wounds. We become beggars, casting aside dignity and exploiting those who care for us when we repetitively describe and display our pitiful "condition."

I had a client, a woman whose third child, a longed-for son, had died of SIDS (*sudden infant death syndrome*) at sixteen months. Her suffering was undeniably genuine, but her treatment was, by my standards, unsuccessful. I never doubted her pain. This woman, Marie, was unwilling to move forward in the grief process by any path I was able to provide. She literally "took to her bed" and became a voluntary invalid.

At the time I saw her, both her daughters and her husband, as well as her mother and several neighbors, were involved in "protecting" her. She had become a petty tyrant, complaining of her great loss and demanding the others' complete devotion. She was frighteningly depressed. Her husband was emotionally exhausted by two years of this behavior. Her daughters had both run away several times, feeling devalued and unloved in comparison to their mother's bottomless, self-serving grief.

Note that I did not say Marie was unable to make progress in her grief work. If I, as therapist, had believed she was incompetent or entirely immobilized, there would have been no basis for attempting expressive grief work. As her therapist, I had to have hope for a positive outcome or I would have been defrauding her of time and money in our sessions. And I did see reason for hope. But my attempts to get her to assume enough responsibility for her emotional condition so that she could take effective action were defeated.

By placing the responsibility to change on Marie, I was not being hard-hearted. I was being respectful of her dignity as a person with considerable potential and resources, including a loving family and good physical health. But in the end, Marie's energies continued to be bound up in the unwholesome mileage she derived from her loss and her refusal to move through her obstinate grief. She did not visibly benefit from the therapy. I believe she could have benefited had she been willing to engage grief as a *process* rather than entrenching herself in the secondary gains she derived from having others organize their lives around her woeful *condition*.

The third characteristic of appropriate grief work is that it cannot be rushed. Simply coming to genuinely *believe* death has occurred is difficult to assimilate. Acceptance cannot come before belief. Neither can we skip the steps of self-disclosure and self-examination that will bring changes—adaptations—to our new, uninvited reality. We will not be able to avoid our confrontation with our faith and view of God. When I say understanding cannot be hurried, I don't mean to promote a wait-and-see approach. In sorrow and grief work, I am an activist.

As feelings emerge, there is no more constructive response than to acknowledge and appropriately express them. The energy of painful feelings needs to be discharged. I have known people who condemned themselves for wishing for the death of a sick partner and, particularly, for longing to be relieved of the burden of care. If peace is to be found, such feelings must be recognized and worked through. I knew a woman whose son had also committed suicide. She had been *sensing* his unacknowledged intention and had felt frantically impotent, wanting to intervene and having no means. When she recognized that among her complex feelings about her son's death was relief at no longer being in this helpless position, she condemned herself terribly. She had to face these emotions when they emerged. Her recognition of the feelings could not have been hurried. Nor could the feelings have been pressed back down without great cost to her psychic equilibrium.

Finally, appropriate expressive grief work must be suited to the individual. We each have our own pace and our own characteristic way of going about the business of life. That I am quick does not mean that another is wrong to be deliberate. It only means that we are unique and will do our grief work differently.

Personal Rituals for Transmutation

How can the roiling emotions of grief and terrible lassitude of sorrow be channeled creatively and wholesomely? The first essential is *a commitment to heal*. This commitment can become an empowering personal myth: "I am a resilient person, able to move through my suffering and find a good life." All inner experiences and new developments in one's world come to be viewed through a lens that highlights the implications for healing, and new choices are made with this purpose in mind. The commitment to heal requires hope. Lacking the commitment to heal, all else is wishful thinking.

I will describe a series of personal rituals through which you may refine, from common sorrow, the pure gold of creative living. It would be wise to try each, no matter how unusual they may seem. How else will you discover new ways of doing life? Each shows you a particular way to focus your attention and direct your energy so that the alchemical fires are more likely to engender a positive transformation. You have come a long way in self-aware discovery by reading and participating in the rituals of this book. Now you are ready to begin the directed healing rituals. They will be strenuous, and your reward will be commensurate with your investment. As my surfer sons say, "Go for it!"

Ritual Twenty-one: Commitment to Heal

When we heal we become able to participate in the activities and engage in the relationships that define an evolving life despite the scarring that has occurred. It is useful to make the commitment that this is your intention. Secondarily, confide in someone who cares about you that you have done so. Following is a suggested "contract" with yourself. Fill in the blanks and don't forget to sign and date it.

Your Contract with Life

I _____, do solemnly promise myself and those I love to heal from the sorrow currently afflicting me. I agree to the following conditions to be commenced on the date given.

1. I will give thought and effort to performing the rituals of this book.

   Date: _____

2. I will make regain my physical strength and vigor to the level it was when I suffered this loss or to an even better state. I know I must take the following steps:(add more letters as appropriate)

   a. _____ Date: _____

   b. _____ Date: _____

   c. _____ Date: _____

3. I will refresh my mind by reengaging in a past interest such as: (list at least three)

    a. _____ Date(s): _____

    b. _____ Date(s): _____

    c. _____ Date(s): _____

4. I will set myself a couple of reasonable, achievable goals for learning something new that has always interested me.

    Date(s):

    Goals:

5. I will actively reach out to three people in a social context, such as having dinner, going for a walk, watching an amusing video, going to an art opening.

    List of folks and proposed activities: Dates:

6. I will open my heart to messages in my dreams, visions, and fantasies that hearten me and record them in my journal. Date:

It is my intention to do the work necessary to have a fulfilling, worthy, and pleasant life.

Signed:

Date:

Now share this contract with someone you trust and who has your best interests at heart. Being accountable is a great motivator when the task is challenging.

All these paths through the flames can be traveled alone or with friends. Since we first sat around a campfire together, groups of people have pooled strength and wisdom, providing comfort and companionship. Therapy and self-help groups can be of tremendous value. I made grateful use of skilled professionals in my grief process, and I believe that counseling is important for many mourners.

Another important and effective element is ritual. Ritual is a way of formalizing and setting apart significant events. It may be used for memorializing (as in the Jewish Kaddish), celebrating (as in Christmas), sanctifying (as in marriage or christening), initiating (as in the bar/bat mitzvah acknowledging that a youngster has come to adulthood), welcoming (putting down the red carpet), or worshiping (the Roman Catholic Mass). In rituals, time is set apart and ceremonies that have deep personal or collective significance are performed. There is a solemn sense of purpose and recognition that the ritual is important. Memories are refreshed, time passed is marked, changes noted, dignity enhanced. Successful ritual is deeply moving and involves a feeling of mystery. At its best, ritual has a numinous quality.

The alchemist's rituals were designed to transmute the base material from its common form to something precious. Each of us must learn, as part of our maturation, to become more adept in directing our life energies. Failure to do so permits the dark, fearsome, passive forces of entropy and decay to take hold. Success means directing energy toward growth. Taking charge of the direction our energy flows is the refining task of our lives. It is our challenge to direct our own energies in order to be survivors of the alchemical fire. A sorrowing person is weary. Sleep comes hard and may be troubled with terrible or restless dreams. Grief saps energy while creating none. An exhausted mind and body distorts reality and alters perspective. By directing one's energies wisely, pleasurable rest will finally, blessedly come. The remainder of this section is devoted to creating personal rituals for developing and directing the energy of sorrow into growth and creativity.

I have, where appropriate, taken a lighthearted tone. This is not to trivialize the work, but to model and encourage smiles and enjoyable experiences. There is much ahead that will stretch your mind and heart, so allowing pleasure to be part of the process will move you toward your objective: a wholesome, full life.

Creative Visualization

Shakti Gawain has written a disarmingly simple book titled *Creative Visualization* (1982) that I frequently recommend. Her language is direct and the pleasant exercises are entirely "do-able." The book makes highly accessible those basic psychological and spiritual principles for developing the capacity to rechannel energy in creative directions.

Each of us can be thought of as a unique energy field. Sophisticated medical technology can measure our brain waves and the electrolytes in our body fluids. Our bodies give off heat and, according to sensitive scientific instrumentation, generate invisible electromagnetic fields. Chinese medicine, through the use of acupuncture and the study of subtle pulses, claims to have demonstrated discrete energy zones and pathways within the body. An individual's particular pattern of energy is as unique as his or her fingerprints, dental work, or blood chemistry. Death is the absence of perceivably *moving* energy.

All creation—from objects to the primary laws of nature—can ultimately be understood in terms of energy. As iron is drawn to the surface of a magnet, so do we either repel or attract different *energy fields* (Eden 1999). The principle behind the "self-fulfilling prophecy" is that we draw to ourselves those conditions toward which we have, in our imaginations, directed our energies. In studies where a teacher was told that a particular student of average intelligence had an exceptionally high IQ, that student excelled. This illustrates the uncanny power of the underlying myths that structure our perceptions and our behavior. The teacher, in believing the student was intelligent, was able to perceive the student's existing intellectual strengths and to foster them.

Our self-image and habitual patterns of thought are products of the way we have directed our life energies. If we believe and act in life-enhancing ways, we will greet the twists of fate with greater confidence and proficiency. We "create ourselves" by interpreting and managing our own energies and the energies we meet in the world. Consequently, it is invaluable in times of trial to have cultivated positive psychological habits such as expressiveness, honesty, and empathy. We need to practice savoring small pleasures and rejoicing in larger ones.

Habit is both a terrible task master and a wonderful conservator of energy. If we had to relearn or rethink each of our routine daily tasks, life would be laborious and uninspired. I can think about writing this paragraph while brushing my teeth. If I didn't have the habit of brushing, I'd have to focus my consciousness on the task, sacrificing both energy and time. Noxious habits, as we all know only too well, are difficult to break. Good habits, like the competent staff of a successful executive, allow us to focus our energies in creative directions and improve the quality of our lives immeasurably. Psychological habits such as disciplined self-examination, honest expression of emotion, and taking measured risks for self-development are valuable beyond price. "Mining the moment" for pleasure is a reflex to cultivate, for it will bring balance in the dark times.

We create our selves and our futures by how we think, feel, and behave. Our actions tend to bring about whatever we expect, so we are best served when *we consciously take charge of our expectations*. We are the sum of our choices.

But, you may think, I certainly didn't choose to have my loved child or life partner die. Of course not. Fate deals each of us a different hand—we're born into comfort or poverty, we are good-looking or plain, we sing gloriously or are tone-deaf. We may be bright or foolish. We are male or female. These are givens. However, within the structure of our particular set of givens, we perceive in our own unique way and we choose our responses. It is what we *do* with our own energy that defines our experience.

If, as sorrowing people, we believe it is our fate to suffer the rest of our lives, the future will certainly be darker. We may even think we *should* hurt endlessly. By fervently *visualizing* perpetual anguish, we create a mind-set that will make affliction inevitable. When taking up fresh challenges, contemplating the future, or facing death, our attitudes and expectations color our perceptions and shape our behavior.

Expectations are formed from experience and fantasy—a blend of remembrance of past happenings and imaginings of what emerging circumstance will bring. *Attitude* is the posture we assume in relationship to what happens to us. We may be spiteful or generous, self-protective or vulnerable, demonstrative or subdued. Though we may be swept along by events we would never have chosen, the way we respond to them is our *self-defining* responsibility. I want to emphasize that your mind-set is a choice, that an individual's internal images have consequences, and that choices and consequences direct energy. It's important to choose wisely.

A first step in making a genuine commitment to heal our grief is to imagine and visualize a fulfilling life for ourselves without the person or situation to which we were so bonded. This is an enormous challenge to our fortitude and creativity. By holding a picture in our mind's eye of good things happening to us—trips to be taken, holidays enjoyed, friendships deepened—we are redirecting our energies. We are taking a critical step forward through the alchemical fire.

Ritual Twenty-two: Pleasurable Expectations

Creative visualization is one of our most powerful tools for directing our energies to positive ends. It is not, however, magic that brings its results without effort or balance. Like all tools, it is latent until used.

A. In your journal, list at least ten actions, circumstances and/or emotional states that you believe to be desirable. My list reads:

1. *Take the dogs for a long walk at least three times a week for the next three weeks.*

2. *Learn all the words, in order, to "Okie from Miscogie."*

3. *Get a new cookbook and try a few unusual recipes.*

4. *Call David and ask for some of his funny memories of our years of friendship.*

5. *Get a massage.*

6. *Excavate the mess on my desk, and see if I can find the surface.*

7. *Get some travel books or get on the Internet and plan a dream vacation, whether it's practical or not.*

8. *Go buy new earrings to match the new dress I'm going to get while shopping with Paula.*

9. *Check out college catalogues and give thought to taking a class in PhotoShop, Thai cooking, or dog training.*

10. *Write a long essay on how it feels to be healthy, productive, happy, and loving. Base it on what I have already experienced and how I intend to shape my life.*

B. Spend at least three minutes with your eyes closed and your breath (remember ritual 1!) supporting your expectations. "See in your mind's eye," "feel with body memory," or otherwise focus on each expectation. Now that's what I call visualizing!

C. Share this list and your visualizing experience with someone.

Without action, creative visualization can degenerate into the pleasant but fruitless exercise of wishful thinking. If I visualize myself as slender while gorging daily, I will not lose weight. If I visualize myself slender *and* eat wisely, get appropriate exercise, and deal with any inner resistance to becoming slender, I will succeed and be happy while doing so. We must provide the conditions for the success of our visualization.

Ritual Twenty-three: Action

This one is simple. Go back to ritual 22 and put a beginning date on each item. Then show the list to your trusted friend again. Ask the person to gently support you holding to your intention. Hey—you're already further on your way!

Meditation

Electroencephalograms reveal a changing array of brain-wave patterns. Shifting from one to another is natural and spontaneous, depending on our activity at the moment. We are in one state when we are engaged in problem-solving. When we listen to music, we switch to another. Creative writing or watching a sunset will produce other patterns. Meditation is associated with a brain-wave pattern that is believed to be helpful to both emotional and physical healing.

Meditation is a vast subject that comes with an exotic reputation. You may be put off by nontraditional spiritual practices, the idea of "losing yourself" in a strange, unknown mental state, or by Zen masters speaking in riddles. A woman in one of my groups thought meditation was a trap set by Satan, and that if she ever experienced it, her soul would be lost. She didn't mind praying, but that, she said, was different.

My reluctance was not as strong as hers, but I certainly was apprehensive when friends first encouraged me to meditate. I had a knee-jerk resistance to the idea. Nor did I believe I could "do" it—I was too rational. These arguments proved to be self-fulfilling, until I learned that a meditative state is really quite natural. Meditative practices need not be at all esoteric. "Meditation," according to Joan Borysenko (1988), "is any activity that keeps the attention pleasantly anchored in the *present moment*" (p. 36).

By this sensible definition, our lives are rich in opportunity for meditation. It is not necessary to have a forest, an altar, or a vast amount of available time. A bubble bath is a meditation when we attend consciously to the delightful sensory details of rainbows in the bubbles, subtle fragrances, our comfort in the warmth, and other pleasures. Shifting our attention to the present moment elicits the "relaxation response," a bodily reflex that is both enjoyable and healing (Benson 1975). We release from our minds the clutter and endless chatter of analytic observation that characterize ordinary waking consciousness. Attending to what we see, hear, touch, taste, and smell is a present-moment activity. When we are in the here and now, we are not troubling ourselves with "what-ifs," vain regrets, or catastrophic visions. We renew our power.

Another dimension of meditation can be discovered by ritualizing the experience. When we select a special place (perhaps a corner of the bedroom used for nothing else), set up an altar, and return to it regularly to focus on our immediate experience, the setting itself activates our search for deeper wisdom. Objects on the altar should have beauty and be meaningful. My altar is backed by a mirror that reflects four candles (one for each of my children), a bird's nest found on a forest walk, seashells, a brass chime, several river stones, and a few precious objects I've been given. A friend has placed pictures of spiritual masters (Jesus, Buddha, Sai Baba) on his altar. Another simply carries a small rock she found on a sacred mountainside in Asia. She touches it with her fingers and recalls the powerful moment she discovered it. By keeping a flower, a shell, or a special picture on your desk at work, you give yourself the opportunity for minimeditations—islands of peace—several times a day.

What is there "to do" in meditating? Meditation requires the release of ordinary intellectual processes. According to one of my favorite T-shirt slogans, "Meditation is not what you think." "Nonthinking" is a tough concept and a strange practice to us who have been rewarded and required to be constantly processing information. We worry that we may not "come back" if we "bliss out," that we will be helplessly vulnerable and perhaps unable to defend ourselves—or maybe go crazy. Nothing like this will happen in a positive meditative state. What we *will* do is rest the ever-active and ever-interfering rational left side of our brain, just as we might rest our aching backs after digging ditches all day.

Periodically, we need to release the Mobius strip of thinking-reacting-judging-considering that is common to waking consciousness. We need to allow the internal critic-commentator an hour off. We are able to come back into ordinary reality instantly when there is need or desire to do so. After fifteen or twenty minutes of meditation, I am calm and mildly elated. My senses are refreshed. Air tastes like mint and colors are brilliant. I am energized and eager to move, usually to dance or walk. Daily concerns are in reasonable perspective, and I think better. Meditation heals me.

There are many methods to achieve a meditative quiet—a state that is associated with positive physiological changes. I'll share one my favorites. I sit on the bank of a creek. I hear the sounds around me in stereo—letting the music of the water run through my head, in one ear and out the other. I breathe consciously, enjoying the effort it takes to empty myself, giving thanks for the moist forest air that enters me. I lean on a tree and experience the mosses under my hands. My eyes wander, tracing the progress of a limb from trunk to twig, following the movements of a hawk, studying a piece of white alder bark embroidered with rust and ocher lichen.

Leaning forward, I see three tiers in the creek. Reflections, whorls, bubbles, eddies, leaves, and water bugs occupy the top level, a fluid canopy. The middle level holds an infant trout nosing sleekly into the current, leaping for a gnat, returning to conserve energy through proper positioning in the flow. I sense a metaphor and let it slide as too intellectual for the moment. The lower level is an intricacy of flat stones in a thousand shades of green, gray, brown, and black against which I see reddish crawdads scuttling on their purposeful, robotic way. At last I am quiet enough to want to begin my meditation. I smile in anticipation, and when I share this moment with a friend, we experience a profound wordless-touchless intimacy.

I sit comfortably erect and lay my hands open, palms up on my knees. I may pick one spot on the rippled water and keep my gaze there, or I may close my eyes, directing all my attention to a certain sound, often my own breathing. Thoughts come circling in like crows at a picnic, but I've learned that they'll fly off on their own if I don't feed them. And if they don't, I return to listening to my breathing or watching the red-brown crawdad walking on a gray rock. Time has no relevance; I am no more aware of time when I am meditating than I am aware of baseball scores in my ordinary life (not at all). My body relaxes without being troubled by my intervening mind's judgments and demands. When I come back to ordinary consciousness, I am intensely aware that I have done something nourishing, something designed into my essence and too long denied.

There are many paths to meditation—chanting, watching a candle flame or the miracle of rainbow light in a prism, or focusing attention on one's breath. T'ai Chi, yoga, and Sufi dancing are common paths "into" that calm and healing space. Meditation may be a private matter or a group experience. I believe any committed person can achieve it.

Generally, a teacher is helpful. This may be a friend, a professional meditation instructor, a spiritual guide, or a book. Larry LeShan's *How to Meditate* (1984) offers an excellent introduction to meditation and an overview of meditative practices. *Seeking the Heart of Wisdom: The Path of Insight Meditation* by Joseph Goldstein and Jack Kornfield (1987) is a sophisticated, engaging and eminently helpful commentary on the topic. *The Miracle of Mindfulness: A Manual on Meditation* by Thich Nhat Hanh (1976) provides a simple and highly personal guide to a form of Buddhist meditation that many Westerners have found to be particularly useful. For beginners, it is challenge enough to keep awareness in the present moment. Later, more complex and life-altering practices will come easier.

Ritual Twenty-four: Meditation

1. In *The Miracle of Mindfulness*, Thich Nhat Hanh suggest something very simple and do-able: *When you wash the dishes, wash the dishes*. If you are at all like me, when you wash dishes your mind is accustomed to wandering off on byways of planning or reflecting rather than staying with the chore. It seems a mindless, rote task. Not necessarily so! Being *mindful* of the water temperature, soap bubbles, movement of the sponge on the surface of the plates, the wrist movement needed to rinse out the glasses, and the effort required to scour the pots is curiously relaxing and centering. I don't have the radio on or engage in conversation during this frequent meditation. When my mind tries to scoot away to the past or future, makes rude comments on meditation, or distracts me with analysis, I simply acknowledge the thought and return to the dishes. Choose either the dishes, bed making, lunch packing, or other simple, hands-on daily task and for a week, give it your full, mindful attention as you perform. Make note of your physical and mental responses.

2. If you can, get outside into a place where there is running water, trees, animals, birds, or other natural things. If this is not practical, find some *complex* object—shell, geode, flower, driftwood, or exquisite, small art object. Settle yourself and do the routine of ritual 1 with your eyes fixed on the tree, bird, or shell. Explore with your eyes and fingers. Discover textures and the way the light plays on your object. *Learn* it. Make note of your physical and mental responses.

3. Get one of the recommended books or another that a friend has suggested. Read it and practice a few of the techniques. Make note of your physical and mental responses.

Mantras

An important tool in expressive grief work is the development of a personal verbal talisman—a "mantra." A mantra is a sound, word, phrase, or sentence that directs and attracts a particular energy. Some meditations use particular sounds or Sanskrit words.

Another term for the sort of mantra used in expressive grief work is "affirmation." The mantra that will most effectively direct your energy will affirm both who you are and who you will be. It focuses power and energy toward self-acceptance as well as toward your desired result.

As affirmations, mantras are always expressed in positive terms. "I will never be late again," has some distractingly negative words. Instead, try something like, "I will be on time." "I won't eat junk food," would be more effective as, "I will eat healthful food." Affirmation mantras should be short, easy to remember, and rhythmic. With a little practice, it becomes natural to compose your own mantra. Use it until you see reason to make another. It's wise to use only one at a time, so you will keep your focus and avoid diffusing your energy. Here are some examples:

- I am a decent woman, worthy of serenity, pleasure, and love.

- I am a peaceful person, able to understand, accept, and grow.

- I am a caring man, growing in spirituality, emotional depth, and prosperity.

People often protest that such statements aren't true, or that to say such things feels false or conceited. This destructive mind-set denies hope and misses an opportunity to constructively direct energy. If we do not have a vision and a belief in positive outcomes, then we live formlessly, reacting to life's contingencies, but failing to actively set a positive direction for our development.

Just as we can "program" ourselves for failure by continual self-criticism, so we can program ourselves for success by taking charge of our own energies. If we feel it is conceited or egotistical to say "I am a good person," we are missing the point that we must invite the changes we want in our lives by opening our hearts and minds to them. If our behavior and habits have been unproductive, it does not mean that we are doomed to perpetuate what was. But first we must *choose* to change.

When we direct our power toward our own growth, we may feel awkward with the unfamiliar practice. But like all habits, it will become easier with repeated application. Anything worth doing at all is worth doing awkwardly at first.

An affirmation mantra defines and shapes expectations. It is wise to test the power of your personal mantra with an open heart, anticipating success. Your mantra should travel with you and provide a refuge when stress or exhaustion causes trouble. It also should be with you when things go right. It should be repeated at least twenty times a day, with full attention to the words, the meaning, and the rhythm.

I like to say mine as I walk, putting emphasis on each word in turn. "*I* am a loving woman," "I *am* a loving woman," "I am a *loving* woman," and so on. The mantra should be the first thing summoned into consciousness in the morning and the last released in dropping off to sleep. It should be said aloud. While saying your mantra in your mind is valuable, there is extra confirmation and potency in actually hearing the words.

Commit yourself to your mantra. When doodling, scribble your affirmation. Sing it in the shower. Write it out and paste it on the mirror in your bathroom and on the dashboard of your car. Chant it. Carve it in wood, inscribe it in clay, paint it with water colors. Chew your food to its wisdom and brush your teeth repeating it. Swim to its rhythm and say it, say it, say it—out loud and in your heart. Make your mantra an integral part of your life, until it is accepted into your essence and you *know* it's true. Then assess where you have come and how you wish to direct your development from there, and consider formulating another mantra.

Ritual Twenty-five: Affirmation Mantra

The basic structure of your affirmation should be this: "I am a (decent) wo/man, worthy of (three qualities you want to invite into your consciousness)." Example: "I am a decent woman, worthy of security, serenity, and pleasure."

Choose a word from this list (or another of your own) if you prefer it to "decent," then substitute.

kind	honorable	loving	intelligent
deserving	thoughtful	gentle	gentle
wholesome	strong	capable	trusting

Choose three words that best fit you from this list, or come up with your own, as long as they are positive. Plug them into the end of the sentence above.

security	insight	abundance	recognition
serenity	wisdom	comfort	appreciation
pleasure	rest	companionship	vigor
peace	energy	understanding	acceptance
calm	delight	satisfaction	love
happiness	creativity	respect	grace

Remember to practice saying your mantra many times a day, in all circumstances. Use all the sensory pathways as you practice: seeing, hearing, saying, moving, touching. Say your mantra until you know it is true and that you are what you've been inviting. Then, if you want, develop another one.

Movement

We are designed to move. We *need* to move. Mobility is necessary for health. It can also be a powerful tool in expressing grief and developing hope. We experience movement through our kinesthetic sense. It tells us our position in space and provides balance. If we do not use the wonderfully complex instrument we occupy, our joints calcify, our muscles atrophy, and our spirits wither.

Any movement can be useful—stretching, walking, athletics, yoga, or aerobics. Dance is a spontaneous, natural, human expression. As used in expressive grief work, dance is a highly individual, unpatterned series of movements, with or without music, that reflects the emotional life of the dancer. We are not likely to call on the discipline and formality of ballet or other highly technical steps unless they are part of our experience. The dance of expressive grief work may involve either the entire body, with large, open movements, or only the hands, trunk, arms, or other part of the body. There is no need to please an audience. Each dance reflects ever-changing feelings of the moment emerging from deep within.

Ritual Twenty-six: Hand Dancing

Norman, a seventeen-year-old musician, damaged his hands seriously in a skateboard accident. Playing guitar had been a passion. He was looking at a concert career before he was hurt. For months, as he experienced surgeries, casts, and rehab, he castigated himself for clumsiness and bad judgment. Getting him to try this ritual was difficult, but it opened his mind and heart to compassion for his injuries. While certainly not a cure-all, it was a strong start on recovery. Norman has settled on the autoharp as his instrument and is once again immersed in music making.

If you are inexperienced or self-conscious about your dancing, begin with hand dancing, done privately. Put on a favorite tape or record, preferably an instrumental piece. Lyrics tend to impose their own structure; the dancing is meant to express your intensely personal experience. Soft light, perhaps a candle in a dim room, causes moving hands to cast long, interesting shadows on the walls and ceiling. These become partners in the experience.

Begin without a preconceived notion of what you will do—simply follow the music and your own impulse, persisting long enough to rest the rational part of your mind and to permit your emotional life to take form in your movements.

Be sure to do this several times. Once you get the hang of it, you will probably want to include your arms, shoulders, and eventually, your entire body. I've added a scarf or a feather sometimes, because it felt right. Expressive movement is also a way of working through and discharging experiences that are too deep, frightening, chaotic, or intimate to describe in words. When I tried hand dancing in my room, I came to a freedom to move as I felt—not as I had been taught or thought "right." In my hand dance, I have cowered and threatened, shaken my fist at the sky, and dug allegorical graves.

Exercise *alone* has been shown to improve the condition of depressed people. In one program at a state hospital where I trained, patients who had been confined to the back wards of mental hospitals, some so deteriorated that they were incontinent and couldn't feed themselves, were required to participate in twice-daily exercise. Their passivity and resistance was massive—the staff had to work hard to involve them in the program. But the patients were kept active until they were sweating and their respiration and heart rates increased.

After two weeks there was marked improvement. They looked and felt better physically, and almost miraculously, some began to respond to the world they had previously blanked out. They became accessible to other treatment. When the exercise program was dropped for lack of funds, the patients returned to their pathological depression.

We are different from those patients only in degree. It is when we are most apathetic that we have the greatest need for exercise—and the most resistance to it. We require physical activity to relieve our tension, get our juices flowing, and stimulate the brain chemistry that enlivens thought. One of the great inducements of extended physical exertion is what is called the "runner's high"—a euphoria produced naturally in the brain through the release of endorphins. Bestirring ourselves from our sad lethargy takes commitment, but the many rewards will encourage us to repeat the experience. Physical movement, appropriate to the condition of the individual, is a central element in the rituals of expressive grief work.

Certain movements and postures are natural to particular situations. When we are in love, our step is bouncy, our shoulders back, and our faces lifted upward. When we grieve, we may be literally bent over under the weight of our sorrow. Our shoulders droop, our chest caves in, our steps are slow and dragging.

I was brought up to be stoic, praised for my self-mastery and admired for my ability to carry through even under difficulties. The highest praise I ever received from my father was that I was a "brave little soldier." The farce that "everything is under control" cost me much pain and three months in bed with degenerative disc disease later in life.

The profound interaction of body, emotions, and mind should not be underestimated. (For more about this idea, try *Imagery in Healing* by Jeanne Achterberg.) When we inhibit our bodies, we also inhibit our emotional range and our intellectual vigor. When we make a positive change in just one system, we are helping all of our systems. The body is a tangible place to begin. It is accessible. You may not know how to lift your depression or increase your optimism, but you can lovingly encourage yourself to move your body and to care for it well.

Sometimes, in movement activities, I've pounded a drum; at other times I've stamped my feet. I've crouched and jumped and rolled on the floor with my arms wrapped tightly around myself. I have spun around and around until I collapsed on a beach, sailed high on a playground swing, and skipped on a city sidewalk. I have exaggerated the rocking, holding posture of a mother comforting a hurt child—and then experienced myself as the child. I have danced in the moonlight, seeking to describe in my motions the horror of outliving my precious son. Always, *always*, I have felt the stagnant, gouging energy move out and life flow into me.

Stretching movements loosen the spine, articulate the limbs, and free the neck, making us more flexible. They are vitally important. As in many new things, we may do best with a teacher. Beware of one who demands a military rigor—the emotions of grief are powerful, but not regimented. "Soft" yoga is excellent, while the broad sweeping movements of free-form dance will meet other needs. Aikido and T'ai Chi are wonderful ways of experiencing the energy of "ki," or the "vital life force." Experiment with moving to your mantra, to music, and to the sounds of the forest and sea. You may have a good time putting movement to some of your creative projections. Environmental tapes or CDs will support this impulse.

Ritual Twenty-seven: More Movement

Please take note: *If any of the suggested movements are beyond your safe physical capabilities, do yourself a favor and skip them!* If you can adapt them to what is reasonable for you to do, then that's a good idea. If, however, you are simply reluctant, feeling lethargic or self-conscious, plow on ahead: the effort will entertain and reward you.

Of the extensive list following, plan to do one (or its adaptation) three times a week for the next two weeks, at least. Experiment with different ones, do some things you never imagined doing. These activities are designed not only to refresh your body, but also to entertainingly engage your mind with do-able challenges. So, try something new, open your mind and awaken your body to good feelings. Go so far as to have fun with these—get a little silly and remember being young, free, and at home in your good body. Remember, we are reaching for pleasure!

Picking Peaches

Stretching is a kindly way to come into body awareness. It does not demand strength or a particular agility, yet as muscles elongate and are stimulated, feelings of well-being follow. This isn't so different from the emotional-mental stretching you're learning to do in other rituals.

1. Stand in your bare feet on a rug, lawn, or sand.

2. Set your feet as far apart as your shoulders.

3. Flex your knees gently a couple of times and do your best to avoid locking them. Locking makes you rigid and compromises agility as well as interfering with energy and movement.

4. Lift your left arm while keeping your right foot flat and rising on your toes of your left foot. Stretch.

5. Tip your head back and reach for a luscious peach just barely within your grasp on the pretty tree you visualize.

6. Now, do the same thing using your right arm and foot.

7. Alternate.

8. Pick a dozen peaches.

Gathering Wild Flowers

This is another sort of stretching since it involves bending and turning as you walk. Remember, you are moving through your sorrow even as you physically stretch in other new ways.

1. In bare feet or in your socks, stand in the middle of the room, on a lawn, or beach.

2. Remember to keep your knees slightly flexed.

3. Visualize a rolling field in spring, covered with a carpet of wildflowers: poppies, lupin, daisies, tulips, daffodils, thornless roses, lavender, ferns—whatever you like—in wild profusion.

4. Feel the weight of a light basket on your arm.

5. Now, wander the field in the bright daylight with just-right sun warmth on your shoulders and pick a large bouquet to bring home for your altar or as a gift to someone you know will delight in them. Pick plenty! Don't be stingy. And enjoy your walk.

Walking Mindfully

Most of us walk too fast to see the wonders around us, so intent on getting somewhere else we lose track of where we are. In the often difficult work of transforming sorrow into creative living and pleasure, mindfulness will serve you well.

If you possibly can, go outside to a garden, park, woods, beach or other pleasant off-the-pavement location.

1. If it's safe, take off your shoes.

2. Stand still, lightly balanced on your two feet, knees flexed, shoulders relaxed.

3. Your mission, should you choose to accept it, is to use your eyes, nose, ears, and willing body to move like observant fog through the landscape.

4. Let your eyes roam, making note of leaves on the grass or sand, shadows, unevenness in the terrain, colors, textures, creatures, juxtapositions, *everything*.

5. Let your nose tell you about the season, what is blooming, what is to be avoided.

6. Listen for bird song, the squeak of sand or snow underfoot, children playing.

7. As you move, match your breath to your movement. Inhale when you move your right foot, exhale as you move the left. Get a pleasant rhythm going. Enjoy!

8. Move in such a way as to disturb things as little as possible (you're fog, after all!)—not a stick, leaf, or blade of grass. You will need to be mindful, move slowly, feel balanced and aware. Walk mindfully at least fifteen minutes.

Swinging on the Gate

Grown-ups often avoid "looking foolish" or "behaving childishly," thereby denying themselves the freedom to experience a whole range of motion and fun that is easily available. In sorrow, it is particularly hard to remember being carefree. You may need this refresher.

A delightful experience of childhood is swinging on a garden gate. Parents object, of course, but the fun is almost irresistible. If you lack a sturdy garden gate to practice with, do not despair.

1. In socks or with bare feet, stand in a doorway.

2. Face the frame (not the door!) and grab it solidly with both hands, about waist height. This is your pivot point.

3. Flex your knees deeply enough that you feel it in your calves and your arms are straight out from your grasping hands.

4. Push your fanny back and swing it emphatically to one side, hanging on to the jamb, keeping knees flexed. Your heels need to be just a tiny bit off the floor so you can shift your feet along with your bottom as you "swing on the gate." Swing your fanny to each side with an increasingly exaggerated flourish. Laugh at the amusing sight you must be, laugh like a child on a gate.

Dancing in the Meadow

Moving to act out a fantasy is good mental exercise as long as you are careful *which* fantasy! Even if you are not young, your body and senses remember youth. Spend a moment recalling some physical exploits of that time of life, thanking your body for retaining the memory of the experience.

Dancing in the meadow requires a partner. A human being is okay, but for our purposes a couch cushion is actually better. It needs to be firm and have a little weight, but nothing that strains you.

Put on some light, "movin'" music: something without lyrics, if you can. Remember as you select it, you're about to go dancing. Wear something in which you can move easily. Back to bare feet or socks in a protected environment.

1. Holding your pillow close to your body, close your eyes and sway to the music.

2. Visualize a lovely meadow in moonlight. The grass and flowers are fragrant. A little creek divides the softly rolling land and chuckles as it cascades over small rocks. Around the far edge is a copse of rustling trees and off to the other side is a view toward a few lights in cottages in the village below. You are entirely safe: there is no danger, no threat. Your body is pliant, eager, and balanced. You are with the companion of your dreams, one who is fully attentive and in tune with your mood of happy anticipation. A full moon lights your way and all is well.

3. Exaggerate your swaying until you have the impulse to take a step.

4. Allow the music to motivate you to dance with your partner in the moonlight, taking pleasure in your flexibility and grace.

5. When the music ends, settle in the grass to catch your breath and enjoy your situation.

Carrying a Basket

An important part of movement is balance. In grief work we often feel "off center" or "wobbly." Physical and psychic balance are parallel. You will have no difficulty in understanding this as you experience "carrying the basket."

1. Find a handless basket, between six and twelve inches in diameter, with a flat or "dished in" bottom. Have a banana or something of similar weight and shape handy.

2. Stand in front of a long mirror on a flat surface with either bare feet or in comfortable, low shoes with feet shoulder-width apart, knees unlocked, and head raised. Drop your shoulders.

3. Do ritual 1. Breathe out *unsteadiness* on the cleansing cycle. Breathe in *balance* on the refreshment cycle. Do this at least four times.

4. Close your eyes.

5. Place the basket on your head in such a way that it stays put.

6. Open your eyes and see the position of basket in relationship to your head, neck, shoulders, and general posture.

7. Take a step to one side. If at any point the basket falls off, pick it up and return to the step before.

8. Turn all the way around.

9. Walk across the room.

10. Return to the mirror.

11. With the basket still on your head, reach up carefully and put the banana in it.

12. Keep watching yourself as you work to get the banana in such a position that you can repeat the movements you accomplished before the load was put in your basket. Keep at it, this can be done.

Even a strange burden can be borne, with balance and persistence. This idea will give you hope and real encouragement about your abilities.

Pulling Taffy

There are always opposing forces working on us. If the sun is out, but work is calling to be done, we feel tugs in different directions. When we are grieving, we certainly feel the tug of entropy—decay—against the pleasant vitality of creative action. This tension is the situation of being human. As we have awareness of these opposite pulls, we are better able to direct our power in life-supportive directions.

1. Get a short (two-foot) bungee cord and carefully wrap the hook ends with well-secured cloth, like dish towels, to make a couple of easy-to-grab handles.

2. Stand as you've learned to do in a solid, yet flexed posture, holding a handle in each hand.

3. Do ritual 1 with this addition: As you cleanse (exhale) *sadness*, pull hard with your left hand, stretching the bungee to its limit, while holding the right end steady.

4. When you inhale (refresh), pull *courage* into your body and let your right hand take over, pulling the bungee the other way as the left hand resists.

5. Do this, alternating, for at least six cycles, observing where the strength is and how resistance develops and then fades.

Slithering Like a Serpent

Whether or not you appreciate snakes for their place in the ecology, it's hard to deny their grace of movement. Action moves through them in beautiful sequence without jerkiness, and their hesitations are totally alert. To know that you, too, are graceful and directed is satisfying.

You will need to be in a hot tub, swimming pool, or other quiet body of water for this activity.

1. Stand or sit until your shoulders are nearly underwater.

2. Extend your arms and relax your hand, wrist, elbow, and muscles. Let them float just below the surface.

3. Touch your thumbs to your index fingers on each hand. These are the snakes' heads.

4. Now, undulate your arms and hands from the shoulder, raising and lowering as impulse suggests, until you have two graceful snakes intertwining and then swimming away. Enjoy this with your eyes as well as your arms.

5. Floating, make similar movements with your legs.

6. Now, involve your trunk, arms, legs, and head in moving through the water with the magical beauty of a water snake in pursuit of gnats. What fun! What smooth motion! Good for you!

Skip to My Lou

Isn't it curious how, for the sake of decorum, we abandon things from childhood and then forget how good they felt? Skipping is an almost universal way of combining walking and running for children when they are feeling good. It is a happy locomotion.

Wear well-fitting shoes with smooth soles and skip ten feet or so, then turn and come back. Notice how your breath is speeded up and you are involuntarily smiling. This is a good antidote for the doldrums. Practice it often, preferably outdoors in the park or down the sidewalk, where you will be setting a good example of retrieving lost pleasures.

Charley Chaplin

Long ago, when I was a child, skipping rope to rhymes was an energizing movement activity. We often skipped to goofy or mildly naughty verses. One I remember is:

Charley Chaplin went to France,
To teach the ladies the hootchy kootchy dance.
Heel and toe,
Knee and elbow,
Turn around turn around.
Wriggle your bottom,
Like a lady of France.

1. Get yourself a good jump rope at a toy store. It needs handles so the rope can turn easily.

2. Find a hard surface, like sidewalk or in a garage.

3. No shyness now—remember, prize fighters jump rope for agility and aerobic exercise.

4. Taking it easy at first, do a little jumping.

5. As you gain familiarity, add a rhyme from your childhood or just count rhythmically.

6. This is great indoor exercise if you have a porch or garage. Enjoy!

Swinging on a Rainbow

I'm going to encourage you now to go outside and find a children's playground. Choose an early morning or late day time, so you will have the place largely to yourself. Usually, there are pipe constructions designed for hanging activities—no, not like in the Old West—hanging from knees (I'm not asking you to do that, either!) or chin-ups.

1. Select a section of the structure where, if possible, you have to reach up to grasp the bar, but your feet are firmly on the ground. If you're too tall, pick the highest and sort of squat to get a pull on your arms.

2. Test your grip and adjust it until you feel solid, still with feet on the ground.

3. Close your eyes and visualize a glorious rainbow. Let it shine, and enjoy the brilliance. Let the bar in your hand take on the colors of the rainbow. Don't worry—rainbows are sturdy while they last.

4. Lift your feet, giving a little push—nothing extreme. Swing.

5. Feel the surprise of your shoulders, the interest of your muscles.

6. Experiment with different strengths of push and with a little rotation of your hips.

7. Let rainbow light suffuse you. How pleasant!

Skating on the Mill Pond

One thing for sure, being in a sorrowing place takes a person to their depths. You may have felt so immersed in "the sadness swamp" that it was almost impossible to imagine normality, let alone lightness and pleasure. Skating, like surfing, requires awareness of the surface supporting you, its quirks and characteristics. Both are wonderful mindfulness meditations, for they hold you in the moment with a not-so-graceful price on being inattentive. They both also offer the sensation of lightness, freedom, and speed.

If you are physically competent to do so, go roller-blading, ice skating, or body surfing. Enjoy every nuance of your smooth motion, your whole-body balance, and enjoyable physicality. Recognize that you are purely in the present—in a nonsuffering state—while you're engaged in skating.

If it isn't wise for you to do the activity in the previous paragraph, do not despair. Wearing a pair of smooth socks, find a bare floor and *simulate* a skater's movements. Once you get the hang of it, close your eyes and ice skate on the canals of Holland or through the most lovely park imaginable. Skating is noted for its speed and smoothness as well as the ability to maneuver gracefully. Music can help, so think about what you'd like to skate in harmony with. You can do this, and it's good for you.

Climbing a Mountain

There are a lot of phrases relating to travel associated with the passages of life. "Find the right path," is a common one, as is "life's a journey." Because you've been suffering, it may feel like you've been in a "slough of despond." Let's put into action another travel metaphor.

1. Go for a walk and find a hill steeper than you ordinarily climb. If you live in a flat place, then use a stairway or a stairstep device at a gym.

2. Before you begin, perform ritual 1. Use the word *fatigue* on the exhalation and the word *succeed* on the inhalation. Do this at least four times.

3. Remember walking mindfully? "Climb the mountain" the same way, knowing that at the summit is a long view on your life and a fresh perspective.

4. If you do not reach the top this time, recognize you have come further than when you started and will doubtless go further next time.

Robin's Nest

Robins are cheeky fellows full of song and intent on the crucial business of getting early worms. They like to nest far out on limbs where predators are less likely to reach eggs or hatchlings. Such limbs swing gracefully in the wind in a soothing and exhilarating fashion. You have been hurting a while and could probably use a nice soothing-exhilarating experience.

1. Return to the playground where you swung on the rainbow. This time, find the swings. Put your adult bottom where you once put your childhood tush. Feels about the same, doesn't it?

2. Push off easily, grasp the ropes or chains firmly, and lean back, pumping with your legs. Get a little altitude and then close your eyes. Be a baby robin in a nest high in a maple tree on a gusty spring day. You're secure, so enjoy the motion and participate.

3. Perform ritual 1 as you swing. Breathe out *fear*, breathe in *excitement*. Good for you!

Owl Vision

Besides relishing a nice mouse snack, flying on silent wings, and never urinating, owls have other unusual qualities. An owl can turn its head almost all the way around so it can look down its own back bone. It has, therefore, a three-hundred-and-sixty-degree view of its environment. Think of this as a metaphor for enlarging your own perspective.

1. Sit upright, spine supported, feet solidly on the floor.

2. *Softly* roll your head in a circle, rather like a heavy flower on a pliant stem.

3. Close your eyes and allow the muscles of your shoulders and jaw to soften as you roll your head.

4. Tip your head back as far as is reasonable for you to do so.

5. Don't forget to breathe.

6. Bend your head forward and see how close you can bring your chin to your chest without straining.

7. Tip your head toward one shoulder, come to center, and then tip toward the other. Don't push. Let the weight of your head provide the momentum.

8. Do these steps four or five times.

9. Open your eyes and softly roll them to one side as your turn your head.

10. Then do the other side. How you doin', Owly? If you work on this one, not only will you develop a fuller range of motion, but your emotional perspective will certainly widen.

Struttin' Your Stuff

Watching people passing by on the pavement or in a mall, unaware they are being observed, can be very instructive. Some appear weighed down by disappointment, some are restless or harried, still others are energized and enthused. It is not just facial expression that gives these impressions, but posture and locomotion. Just notice that the angle of the face to the sky indicates subtle degrees of feelings. The person looking at their feet or just in front of them gives the impression of inwardness, withdrawal, or depression. One with their face forward, eyes fixed ahead, seems goal directed. When the face tips up, we are likely to interpret eagerness or happiness. There are many other body-language cues to emotional states.

Sorrowing people tend to have dropping or braced shoulders, bent necks, slumping spines, and a draggy sort of gait. What is astounding is that a change of posture and pace can materially alter your mood.

Stand up and move to a mirror. What does your body language say about your emotional state?

In succession, still before the mirror but feeling free to move back and forth, simulate the following moods:

a. anger

b. defeat

c. fear

d. hopefulness

e. courage

f. determination

g. intense interest

h. satisfaction

i. pride

j. contentment

It's up to you to choose how your present yourself to others and, particularly, to yourself. Choose a new posture for your next outing. Don't make the mistake of calling it "fake"—instead, call it growth and a willingness to change.

Willow in the Wind

Willows are eager growers, flexible and strong. They are responsive to wind and often sing in a gale like a guitar. Rooted, they are free to wave their limbs and flutter their leaves with reckless abandon, given any breath of moving air.

1. Stand as you've learned to do, with feet wide and knees flexed.

2. Close your eyes and grow roots. Get 'em down there, solid.

3. Test out the flexibility of your main trunk and limbs. Experiment—after all, this is probably your first time as a willow tree.

4. Now, feel a soft August afternoon's warm breeze blow through your leaves, fluttering them.

5. The breeze is picking up and the calendar pages are flying off. It is October, with a gale blowing in. Let your willow body reflect the action.

6. Here it is, mid December, you are leafless and snow is weighing you down, even bending you forward. There is no wind, but it is very cold.

7. Welcome to spring! Balmy zephyrs blow flower fragrances your way, your tender leaves are emerging, along with fuzzy blossoms. Your sap is rising to the warmth and promise as soft sunlight entices you to put on new growth. There is a steady south wind gusting through the woods and up the river, awakening everything. Respond!

Tidal Flow

A characteristic of life is its cellular contraction and expansion. Broaden your view of Earth and see her tides demonstrate ebb and flow in constant melodious synchrony. Being static is unnatural. Even stones alter continually, albeit slowly and in ways invisible to the human eye. Stasis—the balance between opposing directions (up-down, in-out, left-right)—is always momentary. The dynamics of existence are fluid, changing, and we are part of this opening-closing creation.

1. Lie down on your bed or the floor—whatever's comfortable for you.

2. Visualize the ocean shore on a tropical beach. Take time to feel the warmth, smell the ginger blossoms, hear the soft splash of quiet surf spending itself on the white sands. Let yourself become part of the water. Feel the tug of the moon on your surge, the relaxation of retreat to Mother Ocean.

3. Roll on your side and pull your legs up toward your chest while tucking your arms in and ducking your head. Take up as little space as possible. This is your ebbing position.

4. Turn on your back and stretch everything in all directions. Fill as much space as you possibly can. This is your flood-tide position.

5. Alternate these postures several times, allowing yourself to be the water governed by the moon, Earth's rotation, and gravity. Spread yourself out broadly, pull in snugly. Know that these positions are reflective of a universal alternation.

6. If you have long been in a contracted or ebbing posture, claiming little space, attend to how nice it is to flow outward, into the larger world.

Thigh Drumming

Here's an enlivening activity, and you don't even have to leave your chair to do it.

1. Put on some march, rock, or other music with a strong, distinct beat. Anything by Mickey Hart is good!

2. Let yourself get into it, feeling the vibrations through your ears and sharing the pleasure with the rest of your body.

3. When the vibration reaches your hands, begin to drum on your thighs, interspersing hand clapping, if your are so inclined.

4. Don't stint now, bob your head, shake your shoulders, stomp your feet, and drum your thighs.

If you really can't bear to stay in the chair, so much the better. Have a good time, make a small spectacle of yourself privately, but let the magic of the lively tempo speak through your movements.

Swimming the English Channel

Swimming in deep water is a challenging thing. During your time of sorrow you may have felt submerged or had a sense of being "over your head." Distance swimming adds another dimension. To be a distance swimmer takes stamina, dedication, vision, and courage. Try on the idea that your grief process is demanding these qualities of you at this very moment.

1. In a pool or natural body of water, carefully consider your strength and experience to swim a distance you mark off with your eyes. Be reasonable in assessing this, neither taking dangerous risks nor letting yourself off too easy.

2. Swim the distance you've chosen.

3. Rest.

4. Now swim the distance again, but go two strokes further than you really thought you could.

5. Repeat this last step frequently, gradually improving your stamina and surprising yourself. Recognize the parallel in your emotional-spiritual life.

Looking for Faeries

There is a whole lore about faeries, who are not giggling bimbos, tooth collectors, or necessarily dressed with Tinkerbell's provocation. No, indeed. The Little People, as they are called in Ireland, are powerful entities, not to be offended. They are capable of splendidly rewarding those they like. Something (probably a faery) tells me, you're likeable.

This is another combined visualization, affirmation, and movement exercise. Allow at least twenty minutes for it.

1. Go to a natural place—woods, beach, desert, garden, park—on a nice day or evening.

2. Recognize that faeries are not limited to one plane: they can fly, as well as sit still as a tree or hide under fallen leaves.

3. These faeries are in a good mood, without a touch of mischief showing at the moment.

4. There are ten of them within a few yards of you.

5. Your task is reach into the crotch of trees, turn over leaves on the ground, check out the inner spaces of flowers, and generally use your senses to discover their hiding places without startling them. They sometimes disguise themselves as butterflies, sow bugs, or dewdrops. Be alert.

6. Why would you do this? Because each is carrying a small package for you with a quality of emotion or behavior you really need right now.

7. When you find a faery—say, sitting in the glitter of moving water—smile, bow, and hold out your hand. You will almost certainly receive a nicely wrapped box holding smiles, playfulness, serenity, or some other treasure.

8. Keep looking until you find all ten.

That wasn't so hard now, was it?

Asparagus Rising

Asparagus is a tricky vegetable to grow. Not so difficult, given a humus-rich, well-drained soil, sufficient water, and some long, warm days. Kind of like us. The trickiness comes in its pattern of growth. Nothing showing for weeks. Then, overnight, the barest tip of a spear surfaces, hardly noticeable. The next day it can be six inches high and sending out ferny sprigs. Amazing.

1. Lie down comfortably. Think asparagus.

2. Visualize yourself in the secure, well-nourished, fragrant soil of a well-mulched seed bed. You are an asparagus root, waiting for the proper moment for emergence. Meanwhile, you're sending rootlets out in all directions, soaking up nutrient-rich moisture.

3. Gradually raise one or both hands, just a little.

4. At the right moment, pop a finger through the surface into the sweet air of the garden.

5. It's fine to raise a toe and do the same thing further down in the seed bed.

6. Taking your own time, send up spears and ferny growth.

7. Recognize you can be both emergent and secluded. You are asparagus rising!

High Wire Act

When we are in deep emotional-spiritual pain, earlier pleasures and wonders are either entirely out of mind or occasion deeper sorrow for being past. It seems we must walk a delicate line to be in the present without losing track of what we have learned—it's a sort of high wire act. Mindfulness is an enormous help with this.

1. Tension in any part of the body is distracting, so remember to do ritual 1 as you begin.

2. Breathe out *uncertainty*, breathe in *assurance.*

3. Lay a length (about ten feet) of rope, twine, or ribbon straight across a rug, grass, or sand.

4. In bare feet, arms free to provide balance, "walk the wire."

5. Even as you watch your feet, feel your shoulders and arms cooperating in this activity.

6. Remember to breathe.

7. Turn and walk back.

8. Give thanks for your good, cooperative body and mind.

Space Walk

You have courageously looked over this catalogue of visualization-affirmation-movements exercises. I hope you have experienced several and are not only more at home in your body, but feel integrated with your mind. The space walk is simple.

From your refreshed awareness, coming from both mind and body, take a walk through three spaces: your personal space, a natural setting, such as woods, garden, beach, or park, and a gathering place such as a museum, theater, mall, or city street. Do this activity alone, if that is safe and practical. Otherwise, ask your companion to keep a low profile as you do this work.

In each of these places do the following activities, making clear note of how you feel as you "occupy the space" mindfully. *Be* there.

1. Perform ritual 1.

2. Touch a variety of surfaces and objects, attending to their temperature, texture, color, function, and other details.

3. Lay out a "high wire" in your mind, visualizing it in the particular space you're exploring, and walk it carefully.

4. Stop and observe often.

5. Affirm that you are a good person, doing your work, moving through a difficult process and making good progress into a new space in your life.

In the following chapter, "Making Yourself Heard," you will have the challenge of moving your voice, both aloud and in writing, out into the world. Breath, as you've learned, is movement. Speech and vocal sound ride upon breath, in fact, are entirely dependent on it. So, as you've learned to move your hands and body, you are about to learn to move your words and feelings on your breath. This can be enormously liberating.

CHAPTER 6

Making Yourself Heard

I have been here before,
But when or how I cannot tell
I know the grass beyond the door
The sweet keen smell
The sighing sound, the lights around the shore.

—Dante Gabriel Rosetti

Snuffle, grunt, yawn, sigh, sob, gulp, cough, sneeze, hiccup, cackle, pant, whistle, smack, growl, scream, whine, wail, keen, hum, chant, groan, chortle, giggle, laugh, howl, snarl, sing, intone, whisper, cry, speak, choke, gag, retch, yell, screech, gargle, trill, praise, lament—these are words of action. In this case, each verb describes an action for the human voice. Of course, we also make personal sounds by clapping our hands, gnashing our teeth, cracking our joints, and expelling flatulence. We are sound-producing creatures.

Part of becoming "civilized" is to learn which behaviors are and are not "polite." We learned, early and too well, what is "correct" in the sounds we may produce.

Don't belch at the dinner table.
Ladies keep their voices down.
Stop yelling at your sister.
Look twice, speak once.
Be quiet around your betters.
Children should be seen and not heard.
Whistling girls and cackling hens always come to the same bad ends.

In learning so well, we have had to deny that we even feel the inner stirrings. We were trained to repress our noisy, expressive sounds. Tragically, we have lost part of ourselves in the process.

In learning these "civilizing" inhibitions, we had to constrict our throats, immobilize our chests, make our breathing shallow, and block our feelings. As adults, we are frightened by the emotional sound of our own voices. We stifle our groan of pleasure in love making, block the scream of terror when startled, or censor our wail of profound sorrow. We have forgotten the full and natural use of breath and voice we knew as children. In my own life, long ago, the only time my then-husband heard me pass gas was when I was in child-birth—I apologized! Maybe you can identify.

Ritual Twenty-eight: Making Sound

Maurice was normally a quiet man, seldom raising his voice. When his family home burned, all the mementos and familiar places of his life were destroyed in an hour. It took him longer than many people to become vocally expressive. Later, he said, "Once I could croak out 'I'm pissed off!', it was as if I found the volume knob, and all I wanted for a while was to play with it."

To unlock your throat and move sufficient air through your body in order to make your-self heard is often an intimidating matter. Years of habit and training are like vises on our throats. We are afraid we'll be heard. How strange! What a disservice to a perfectly natural act: personal expression. You will likely want to find a way to be alone as you first practice this ritual. Another possibility is doing it with a young child, who will be a good model and add to the enjoyment of finally getting your voice back.

Use this ritual not only for its serious and important purpose, but for the pleasure of the activity. Have some fun again, you're due!

- Snuffle like a piggy smelling fall apples.

- Grunt like an old man sitting down in a too-low chair to read the paper.

- Yawn until your ears almost fall in.

- Sigh deeply and loudly.

- Gulp as if you are eating and must finish a whole plate of strawberry shortcake in three swallows.

- Cough two ways: as if you're in a theater and don't want to disturb anyone, and as if you had a feather in your throat.

- Burp: maybe you'll have to really fake this, but pretend out loud you have swal-lowed too much soda water all at once.

- Cackle: first cackle like a startled hen who has just laid a paisley egg, then cackle like a happy witch stirring her pot of newts and toad toes.

- Pant: you have just run the first three-minute mile, uphill.

- Whistle: try a variety of sounds like a wolf whistle, at a ball game, and calling a dog.

- Smack your lips: Man! Those cookies and milk taste better with some satisfied smacking, don't they?

- Growl like a lion, a crabby old woman on awakening, and/or as an expression of frustration.

- Scream: imagine you came around the corner of your bedroom door and saw a full grown ostrich sitting on your bed. Or, if that's too hard, as if you're in a movie like *Alien* and something weird comes out of the woodwork.

- Whine: be three years old and try to talk someone into giving you more candy than is good for you.

- Hum: try "Happy Birthday," "Polly Wolly Doodle All the Day," or something cheerful.

- Groan: try these three ways—as if you had overdone it at Thanksgiving dinner, as if you were balancing your checkbook, and when your team loses.

- Chortle: this is a rather smugly pleased sound, expressing satisfaction.

- Giggle: something has really—maybe literally—tickled you.

- Laugh: you can do it! Remember a good joke, a funny situation or a ridiculous piece of business.

- Howl: be a wolf on the Arctic tundra at full moon in June. Alternatively, exaggerate the sound in a country song, preferably by Hank Williams.

- Snarl: somewhere in you is a hint of junkyard dog or protective animal. Let its sound out.

- Sing: let loose with a song from childhood or when you felt young and exuberant.

- Whisper: tell a juicy secret or funny story to someone in this confidential manner.

- Yell: take yourself in memory to an exciting sporting event and holler for your favorites.

- Screech: make two sounds—an alarmed owl and a really rusty gate hinge.

- Gargle: take something you like into your mouth, like apple juice or warm cocoa, gargle and, being a little naughty, swallow it.

- Praise. Most of the other parts of this ritual have been designed to help you smile again as well as open your throat to your own sound. In this last one, open your heart as well as your throat and throw verbal gratitude at the sky in a gesture of appreciation.

As we reclaim our breath and voice, we draw air into our chest and consciously release it. Focused awareness on breath and voice vibration is a central technique in many meditative practices and can lead us to greater release in our emotional expression. Such awareness is calming, centering, and satisfying. Remember ritual 1? This is the perfect time to revisit and refresh.

Breath supplies us with oxygen to fire our metabolic furnace. Just as importantly, it carries away the by-products of combustion. When we are in the alchemical fire, if our grief is to be transmuted to creativity and pleasure, we must rid ourselves of wastes and unfinished business. The cleansing power of breath is tied to sound.

Appropriate expression in grief work discharges negative energy. As a psychotherapist, I put the utmost value on expressive sound. When a woman who is furious though inhibited can sound authentically angry, I know she is well advanced in her emotional work. When the sounds are accompanied by convincing expressive movement, then I know she is far along in transforming the terrible burden she has been carrying. A variety of vocal forms may be called upon in expressive grief work:

- Keening: a lamentation for the dead uttered in a loud, wailing voice or sometimes in a wordless cry. In Ireland, China, Crete, Mexico, and among the Eskimos, old women perform this duty to the dead—calling out the tones of misery in shrill, penetrating voices.

When my friends Bob and Zora came to my house, I knew by their faces that something was terribly wrong. My first question was, "My son or yours?" I don't know where that intuitive flash came from. When Bob said, "Patrick," everything froze for a microsecond. Then my voice filled the room with an animal wail that was utterly foreign to my experience. I had uttered the "wordless cry" and surrendered to loud keening.

Though I didn't recognize it for a long time, that was my first discharge of negative energy. I believe I would have died of horror if I hadn't wailed. Though I keened again and again, never did I touch the raw reality of that first, instinctive cry of a mother whose son had died. It was primitive, uncalculated, rending. I had begun my grief process.

• Weeping: to express deep sorrow by shedding tears.

I had as a client a retired Navy captain whose wife of forty-plus years had died suddenly of a heart attack. He sat looking at me tensely while complaining of depression and insomnia. Captain Holbrook had carried out all the "proper" activities. He'd arranged a good funeral, dispersed his wife's belongings to their daughters, sold the house, rented an apartment, and gone out socially. Despite these appropriate behaviors, he was losing efficiency in his new job. He did not enjoy the women clamoring for his attention, had lost his fascination with golf, and "just couldn't sleep" without a tumbler of Old Bushmill's whiskey.

It emerged that he had never shed a tear. After all, Navy captains don't cry. Not until he finally permitted his feelings of "lost aloneness" to come to consciousness could he cry. Feeling abandoned came when he recognized the little child in himself and the despair he felt at his wife's death. With his tears came anger—at God, at colleagues with living partners, at being "cheated."

The night he cried, he slept unmedicated by whiskey. With more expressive grief work, he was revitalized. His life took on savor, and he became expressive in other ways. The alchemical fire had altered his perception, and he became more emotionally responsive. He remarried three years later and invited me to the wedding. I cried all through the service.

As a therapist, I'm on the alert when a bereaved client doesn't weep. The swollen eyes, runny nose, and gasping breath of hard crying vividly show the energy involved. After Patrick's death, I feared that if I began to weep, I might not stop. For several weeks I was subject to uncontrolled spasms of sadness. I called these "grief attacks." Tears would start flowing down my cheeks at work, in the bank, on the street, in a restaurant, and any time I heard Bach. I would wake up crying and I cried in the shower.

Working with a therapist, I discovered that I had a deep well of regrets, unbestowed blessings, fears for my living children, guilt over my role in Patrick's death, and the death of my husband Joe—all of which overflowed in wordless tears. I was ready for my next step.

• Lament: crying out in grief. The Lamentations of Jeremiah is an Old Testament text for howling aloud one's sorrow, anger, and desolation. In chapter 3, Jeremiah laments:

I am the man that hath seen afflictions . . .
He hath led me, and brought me into darkness, but not into light.
Surely all is against me . . .

He turneth his hand against me all the day.
My flesh and my skin hath he made old; he hath broken my bones.
He hath builded against me . . .
[All is] gall and travail.
. . . set me in the dark places as they that be dead of old.
He hath hedged me about, that I cannot get out.
He hath made my chain heavy.
Also when I cry and shout, he shutteth out my prayer.
He hath enclosed my ways with hewn stone.
He hath made my paths crooked.
He was unto me as a bear lying wait, and as a lion in secret places.
He hath turned aside my ways, and pulled me into pieces; he hath made me desolate.
He hath bent his bow, and sent me as a mark for the arrow.
He hath caused the arrows of his quiver to enter into my flesh.
I was derision to all my people . . .
He filled me with bitterness, he hath made me drunken with wormwood.
He hath also broken my teeth with gravel stones, he hath covered me with ashes.

There is more. Jeremiah's sense of abandonment and misery are there to read. Thousands of years later, they are the voice of the sufferer in the alchemical furnace. To me, they are familiar complaints. In time, I came to unburden myself of my grievances against my fate, my antifaith, my family. Expressing my laments was a powerful experience, and I recommend it in protected circumstances: with a counselor, in your journal, or with an absolutely trusted friend who won't try to quiet, moderate, or counter your expression.

Why do this? Why indulge in an orgy of self-pity, blame, and complaint? What good will it do? And doesn't lamenting work against creative visualization? How could lamenting do any real good, since it summons up all that blistering suffering? Wouldn't facing so much pain destroy a person? With these and other fears, we seek to avoid the resentful, confused forces within us.

To contain our wails and complaints, we use great amounts of energy, which is then unavailable for creative living. We must discharge what is hurtful. We will make space for other emotions and free the energies that had been devoted to containing the pain. When we are effective in discharge, we unburden our psyches of graceless misery rather than holding it inside like a growing canker.

Sometimes people fear that they are manufacturing or being incited to perform in a way false to their own nature. Often feelings of grief are so terrifying, or their expression is so foreign, that a sense of unreality accompanies the rituals. It is my experience that only the extremely rare, narcissistic person enjoys wallowing in his or her misery and wringing concessions out of others. The majority of us are authentic when we wail out our inner turmoil. It takes courage to break through the habit of inhibition. It is well worth it to begin to move the stagnant energy tied up in frozen emotions.

We must express our outrage, confess our sins of commission and omission, and symbolically rend our flesh and tear our hair if we are to empty the foulness and abandonment we feel. We choose our time, place, and companions well, and we "empty out" to be rid of such emotions. If we deny these feelings, they become like sea worms boring through the wooded hull of a boat. In their silent action, they can destroy us.

We had best begin our lamentations with a clear affirmation that we will complete our old business as a result of expressing these negative emotions. Thus, we accomplish several purposes. First, the energy that has been used to fend off expression will be freed to serve us better. The day after my first therapy session following Patrick's death, I was able to walk a half mile without back pain. I attribute this to the release of my emotional tension.

Second, though the process may be as unpleasant as vomiting a bad oyster, the resultant relief will repay us many times over. By giving up bitterness—heaving it out—we cleanse ourselves. The evil potions of fear and loathing will be cleared from our systems. *We must take care not to gather the poisonous feelings up again—we must visualize them gone!*

For myself, using the tools of creative projection, movement, and sound, I visualized my grievances as stones. They were in an imagined army-green backpack, many times too heavy for me. I was bowed under the weight, my "brave little soldier's" back nearly broken. I threw the first stone, marked "husband," and felt better. I did this work with a therapist, and by the time I had "thrown all my stones," I was exhausted with the clean fatigue of someone who has worked hard. I could stand up straight again and look toward the horizon.

To lament is to actively express difficult emotions, unreasonable ideas, and our most unlovely parts. It is to beg, bargain, and, eventually, accept life as it is presented. It is to cleanse and empty. This is necessary to move forward through the alchemical fire.

Ritual Twenty-nine: Lamentation

Using Jeremiah's model, draw up your own list of complaints against fate, luck, or whatever else you feel has brought your current unhappiness on you. It is critically important that, as you do this, you visualize emptying out the misery and stagnation from your body, mind, and spirit. I have often used one of two images to facilitate this. Imagine a vat of really dirty, turbid water with a nasty scum on it, which is the reservoir of your resentments and suffering. Each lamentation is a pail emptied from the container. Stay with it until you empty the whole miserable thing. Alternatively, visualize and experience yourself carrying a backpack of heavy, dull stones. As you write your lamentations, throw or drop one out of the pack until you can stand upright again and move forward lightly. This is hard, worthy work that will reward you with a refreshing sense of buoyancy.

- Sigh: to release a wordless exhaled breath expressively. To draw in a deep breath means we must make room in our lungs by expelling the stale air already there. We attempt to suppress our feelings by holding or limiting our breath. Imagine yourself in the dentist's chair, waiting to feel the pick scraping a crumbling filling. Chances are you held your breath, seeking to minimize the pain. Imagine yourself in an intersection, in a stalled Volkswagen, with a log truck closing in on you. Chances are you held your breath. Fritz Perls, originator of Gestalt therapy, said, "Anxiety is excitement minus oxygen."

  My friend Don is slow-spoken, careful with language, but he should have a Ph.D. in Oral Expression for his sighing. When he's entangled with tedious tasks, he nearly moans; when exasperated, it's more of a grunt; and in moments of excitement, the gusts have an eager tone. The sighing Al Gore did during the 2000 election debates were variously interpreted as boredom, arrogance, or impatience; only Al knows for sure, but there was no question that he was emptying himself of something.

When we are first grief-stricken, our pain is overwhelming. We literally feel we cannot bear it. We must buffer ourselves and only let our feelings seep through cautiously. Though holding the breath is an unstudied attempt at self-protection, it does not serve our long-term purpose since it stifles our energy and stops the process of grieving.

Ritual Thirty: Sighing and Yawning

Sighing is your body's effort to obtain oxygen and express feelings. An excellent expressive grief exercise is to sigh several times with increasing intensity and an open-throated sound. Prolong the sound until there is no more air you can push out. The relief is tremendous. Do this four or five times a day. I did (and do) mine in the shower. I feel revitalized and open afterward.

Yawning is wonderful, too, if the yawner doesn't stint on the expressive tone. Give yourself a wide-mouthed, slack-jawed, eye-squinting, rib-stretching yawn or two. Don't forget to make a good loud noise, maybe a glad groan.

- Sing: to vocally sustain notes in harmonic pattern. In Psalms, the people are exhorted to lift up their voices in joyful sound. My client Hazel began a major change of attitude and perspective when she joined a gospel choir. The drab depression she'd lived with since her parent's divorce was no match for the exuberant, passionate power of the music. She discovered that joining her sound with others produced something greater than any one voice alone. From this she took comfort and felt herself to be a participant in an art form, a healing experience.

I am one of the people Garrison Keillor, on the radio program "A Prairie Home Companion," called the "singing impaired." Like many of my kind, I love to sing and am shyly inhibited about doing so in public. Being able/willing to sing marked progress in my grief work. A friend, Marlin, came to my home while I was in my deepest mourning. He played and sang the Beatles' song "Let It Be" perhaps fifty times. The song, a favorite of Patrick's, had deep meaning. I sang some of its wise words and my wandering pitch was unimportant. I felt I was getting advice from my son through the moving lyrics and hymn-like melody.

In the intervening years, I have found that for many other grieving people, vocal music is wonderfully apt for expressing feelings. Singing the songs that were shared with the person who is gone may elicit tears or smiles. It helps heal the survivors. Singing changes moods. I maintain that it's not possible to be depressed while singing "Polly Wolly Doodle All the Day" or "Feelin' Groovy." Bright rhythms, familiar words, and a bold approach can mark a definite turning point in grief work. When we choose "Here Comes the Sun" or "Amazing Grace" to serenade the freeway or to echo in the privacy of the shower, we are truly "getting better." When we risk singing with others, we are infused with their enlivened energy, fostering a lovely companionship.

Ritual Thirty-one: Singing

If, in your life, you have been able to sing easily, then you will find this ritual easy. Choose a song that either has meaning to you or that is lighthearted. Sing, if at first softly, then increase your volume. Fill your chest with air and let it flow out.

If you are a little shy or uncertain about your singing, gather your courage and your breath and begin by singing something like "Mary Had a Little Lamb" or "Row, Row, Row Your Boat." It doesn't matter as long as you make your sounds. Later, stretch yourself by singing along with a CD or tape to something simple and pleasant. I do this stuff in the car and have no worries about such niceties as pitch or key.

- Chant: a rhythmic, monotonous utterance or song. Chanting has long been used to evoke a sense of God's presence. The splendid Gregorian chants of monastic Catholic orders have the awesome power to bring about a sense of wonder and spirituality. The resonant "Om" of Eastern religions sets up a vibration in the head and body of the chanter that flows seamlessly into a meditative state. "Shabbat Shalom" is chanted in Jewish temples every Friday night with a joyous cadence, reminding people that the day of rest and contemplation has come. Shamans the world over chant to alter and deepen their perception of the hidden world. Chanting may lead to the heightened awareness, serenity, and joy of the mystic's rapture. Chanting a mantra or your affirmation will add meaning; to use breath and sound is deeply confirming.

The blending of one's own voice with others can be a high experience. The relentless continuance of a chant taxes a person's stamina. It takes energy and commitment to chant, but it becomes natural once shyness is overcome. Depending on the cadence, chants may be worshipful, mournful, jubilant, or calming. To chant in nature is particularly beautiful, a complete meditation.

Ritual Thirty-two: Chanting

If you have not been accustomed to chanting or have not heard it, a good support is to get a few tapes or CDs of Gregorian, Tibetan, or Native American chanting. As you become familiar, join in. Otherwise, create your own. I like experimenting with a single sound like "om," "ah," "oohw," or "dah." Any of these can be shaded with nuances of feelings. The trick is to choose a pattern of sound ("a-b-a" or "a-a-a") and repeat the frequency for a long time—twenty minutes—while allowing a hypnotic consciousness to emerge. This will alter your perception in a useful way.

- Toning: a voice wordlessly sliding up and down the scale, holding an interval, falling off, growing softer, then louder, is toning. The monotonous, repetitious rhythm of chanting is not present; toning is solely emotional vocal sound. Sustaining and improvising sounds means breath, consciousness, choice, and improvisation. It is, above all, an expression of emotion. A kind of emotional and spiritual clarification comes with toning, as if light is entering the soul.

All children tone, playing with sound. So do jazz musicians. No melody is needed. The voice is an instrument, as much as a violin or a saxophone—it does not need a beat, tune, or words to be expressive. Strange and wonderful harmonies develop when people sound their emotional tones together.

Ritual Thirty-three: Toning

Choose a sound that is not associated with a literal meaning or word. Play with it in your throat. Elongate it. Shorten it. Sustain it. Experiment. Persist for at least ten minutes, rest, then repeat. You will be able to express things that are beyond words. Empty those painful feelings out in this way and be renewed. Tone pleasantly—even joyously.

Throughout this book, I have emphasized the value of breath consciousness and emotional expressiveness. Words and wordlessness each have their place in the sounds of expressive grief work. Yelling, screaming, and commanding are legitimate ways of expression; so are complaining, confronting, taunting, laughing, shouting, and praising. Do not deny yourself the wholesome healing that may be derived through the use of expressive sound.

CHAPTER 7

Finding Your Words, Drawing Your Lines

I shook . . . habit off
Entirely and forever, and again
In Nature's presence stood, as I now stand,
A sensitive being, a creative soul.

—William Wordsworth

Creative projection is my term for a method of recognizing, understanding, managing, and exorcising repressed feelings. It is based in Gestalt and Jungian practices. In creative projection, you work with dream images or other symbols by "becoming" the symbol, speaking as the symbol, and enacting it. Some feelings are beyond words. I may describe the blistering, scouring, scalding pain in my heart when I heard of Patrick's death—but those words are inadequate or even false compared to the intensity of my feeling. By working in clay, a medium that requires no spoken language and which is responsive to every nuance of touch, I was able to work out—and creatively project—my experience. By discharging the stagnant energy trapped in my hurting body, I felt release, understanding, and the satisfaction of having done something that had once felt almost impossibly difficult.

It may well be that all creative endeavor is some sort of projection. Certainly a tenderly prepared meal is a creative projection of the cook. Dance, painting, ceramics, music, drawing, building, poetry, gardening, massage, even mending jeans, are statements about the doer. We are instructed by our own productions, especially when we can escape our bullying self-judgments.

I would like to take the example of my clay work to demonstrate one way to use creative projection. Keep in mind that though I worked in clay, others might substitute a different technique that permits spontaneous, unstudied expression. The mind-set needed is one of openness to the process. There is no requirement to produce "art" or a functional, lasting product.

My moist clay responded to the subtlest pressure, opening itself before my fingers, taking imprints from the wooden plank I worked on. Tearing off a chunk the size of a grapefruit, I made a ball, pinched out a couple of ears, modeled a nose, and pressed eye sockets in the surface. Under my hands a semblance of a face grew—it was no one I knew. I lost patience and smashed the clay into a pancake, only to have a sense of loss. I reformed the ball, working human-proportion features on it again. The face that appeared the second time was fearsome—a monster with a witch's hook nose, sunken eyes, and a snarl on her mouth. I was horrified that I had made such a hideous creature.

Holding the witch, I gathered my courage to discover what part of me she represented. I had formed her out of featureless clay; she was clearly a projection of myself. What follows is an example of dialoguing. It is a verbatim sampler from my journal, six weeks after Patrick's death. I ask for tolerance at the blasphemous, gutter language.

One of the basic tools of my professional practice is Gestalt therapy. The abbreviated definition is that "gestalt" in German refers to "full," "entire," "complete," in a way implying that a thing is more than the sum of its parts. Example: A lawnmower, disassembled, is a collection of gears, bolts, blades, and wheels. Put together, it has a function none of the individual pieces possessed. In Gestalt therapy, the assumption is that we are a collection of parts that, when well coordinated, is greater than any one alone. That is, a good body is even better when inhabited by an aware mind and directed emotions.

An aim of the Gestalt therapist is to bring the client into conscious integration of the elements of personality. The ideas lean heavily on staying in the present moment, speaking in the active voice, and using simple linguistic tools as outlined in the text following.

Note, too, that in Gestalt therapy, the word "it" can generally be changed to "I" or "me" to more closely approximate emotional truth. I hope this brief and incomplete explanation will make the items in parentheses below more comprehensible—they were reminders to myself.

April 11—Evening

I've been staring at this wad of mud sitting on a paper plate on the desk for half an hour. I want to smash the damn thing—it is (I am) hideous.

Me: Christ, but you're an ugly witch— I can't believe I made you.

Witch: You did more than make me, you *are* me.

Me: To hell with that! You're mean looking—hateful—cruel. You're like something that has possessed the clay.

Witch: I repeat—I am you—cruel, ugly, and hateful.

Me: That pisses me off. . . .

Witch: And angry.

Me: Angry? Well, maybe a little, but I'm nothing like you.

Witch: Try it on for size, as you so glibly say to your clients.

Me: Try what?

Witch: And stupid. You're ugly, hateful, cruel, angry, and stupid.

Me: *(Sullen)* This isn't getting anywhere. I don't see any good coming out of this aimless name-calling. *(Turn away)* This is going nowhere—I'm going to quit this asinine dialogue.

Witch:	Good! Leave me in charge, will you? I like that—I can show up in your dreams and in any work you try to do.
Me:	Look, you're not in charge. I can smash your ugly face any time I want. I can damn well dissolve you—you're mine.
Witch:	Exactly. I'm yours. You.
Me:	Part of me, maybe. I hate to admit it. But, you're not all of me.
Witch:	I can twist you any time I want—right now, for instance.
Me:	Damn you! Now I'm really angry—I'm a responsible person, and I'm sick of you. *(Makes threatening gesture.)*
Witch:	Go ahead—what else are you angry about?
Me:	I'm mad at politicians, exploiters, users, the rape of the earth—incompetent therapists—
Witch:	Now we're getting to it (me). Any particular incompetent therapists?
Me:	God damn it! Me. If I were any good, Patrick would still be alive.
Witch:	That's grandiose. Who the hell do you think you are to be holding another person's life—even your own son's—in your control? Don't you believe any of the stuff you've been preaching about personal responsibility?
Me:	Get off my back! Of course I believe it (me)—except . . .
Witch:	You don't believe you could have saved him if you were a better therapist, do you?
Me:	Or better mother. *(Tears.)*
Witch:	Bawl if you want, but unless you face up to how righteously angry you are, I'm in charge.
Me:	*(Taking a deep breath)* I know it. I've known it all along, but God! It (I) hurts.
Witch:	*(Unsympathetic)* Tough. Who are you really angry at?
Me:	Pat! If I had him here, I'd blister his ear! How dare he make a mockery of the years of love, the support—his own potential.
Witch:	Take his picture from the drawer and tell him.
Me:	Do I have to?
Witch:	No. You can leave me in you, eating away at everything, poisoning your work, screwing up your relations with the kids. Be gutless; it (I) feeds me.
Me:	I hate you. I really hate you—or me. *(Takes picture out—looks at it—weeps.)*

Hello, my Beamish Boy. I'm hurting over you. It's your fault I'm hurting. I'm not about to say goodbye. I keep repeating that—selling myself? I can live without you—I already have for six godawful weeks, you son of a bitch. That's funny. Makes me a bitch. I am alive, and you are ashes on the ocean.

Your memorial is in things—leather-bound books, the turquoise hippopotamus from the Met, letters, and bunches of dried flowers in my memory book. Not enough, Pat, not nearly enough. Where is your diploma from Yale, the grandchildren, the books you were to write? You left me your journal and I haven't the courage to read more than a line at a time. I see the pages and know your live hand touched them, your fine mind formed the phrases, your despair colored the sentences.

Your letter said, "Forget me, forget me." Damn you, kid! I didn't try to direct your life, and you can forget trying to direct mine! I love you. I remember you. You are my boy and my pride and my shame. I didn't control your body or soul—leave mine alone. I won't be dismissed by the likes of you. Goddamn, Pat, please let this be a dream of unendurable length. Wake me up! Hold me. Laugh at me. Mock me. Enlighten me. Show me your new book.

World! I hurt! I choose to hurt—don't ask me to play myself safe and mild and cool. No. I'm rocking with pain. I'm breathing hard, my neck is straining—I hurt! I want my child. I'm screaming at you, "Give me back my child you rotten withholders of life." You aren't listening, and I'm in pain, and I won't make your life easier by quitting my pain. Don't force the platitudes of Hallmark cards and chicken soup on me. I'm better than that. I will be done with Patrick—with you, son—in my own good time. This is my statement: I will live, and in living I will commit myself to pain. My joys are mine, too. Katie and Aaron are playing—she's a superb mother! Peter has outgrown another belt. Stan's earache is better, and the surf is comin' up. I am a hub—a vortex. I do know that deferring experience—whether pain or love—is foolish and not my style at all. I don't know enough. I don't know where to go to learn more. I do too know where to go to learn more—ahead!

I'm angry, Patrick Joseph-Elliott Pleskunas. Angry at you. How could you give up? Because I taught you that you belonged to yourself? What a miserable distortion. Because you despaired and didn't share, didn't ask for help, didn't come home, didn't trust. You had no right—no right at all to distort my universe and to give such a message to Katie, Stan, and Peter. Didn't your father's self-murder show you the havoc death can bring? Why were you so angry, so hopeless, so foolish?

It was with this journal entry that I mark the first self-directed progress in my grief work. By reclaiming the ugly, angry, stupid witch in me, I sapped her power, expressed her venom, began her exorcism from my being.

The process of engaging in dialogue, illustrated here in my journal excerpt, is a useful way to learn the dimensions and strength of emerging parts of your personality. Conscious dialogue gives voice to the varied and competing parts of ourselves. Implicit in this process is the idea that what we produce, think, feel, and intuit *is us*. The apple pie I bake or the evil witch I sculpt takes on my particular energy. They come from me. Additionally, we have a range of impulses and needs clamoring to dominate in every situation. Will I be a responsible adult trudging off to work or a happy truant escaping duty to lie in the sun on a warm spring morning? How I settle the conflict directs my day and defines my personality.

We are affected by things, people, and circumstances. It is reasonable to dialogue with them to define our positions, confirm our decisions, and test our options. Throughout the dialogue, we must take care to observe which side of our brain is more active—the "logical" left side or the "emotional" right side—and to be sure that each has its say. The more real and less stagy we become, the more insight comes from dialoguing. Our language becomes less calculated. We are less "fair" and more honest. We deliberately bare our faces, discarding our masks, with the intention of changing for the better.

The dialogue with Patrick's picture felt as if I were talking to him. This sense of "making real" those people or objects with which we have business is important. The dialogue must wring feeling from us—must plumb our darkest depths, must flow as unguarded conversation can flow. Dialogue is a way of encountering parts of our experience hitherto hidden from us.

Creative projection is a tool to be used in conjunction with art materials, dreams, sound, and movement. What we can imagine, we can use to our own ends. Dialoguing with the creations of our inner lives is a powerful way of discovering your unclaimed parts, exploring your darker sides, and working with your dreams.

Ritual Thirty-four: Creative Projection Dialogue

You can follow the model of my work with my witch with any creation of your own. This can be challenging and sometimes frustrating or awkward, but when done effectively, it will be enlightening.

Using a journal is often a good place to begin this dramatic work. Remember to stay in the present tense, active mode, in the first person (for example, "I am Peg's calm part"). Persist even if the going gets awkward or seems a dead end. If the idea of doing a dialogue with a creative expression seems too difficult at the moment, please trying a couple of the following pairings for the work. It is a worthwhile skill.

- Hopeful You—Despairing You

- Perfectionistic You—Laid Back You

- Young You—Mature You

- Courageous You—Fearful You

- Angry You—Accepting You

- Greedy You—Generous You

- Regretful You—Satisfied You

or come up with your own pairing.

Journal Work

The journal excerpts in this book were obviously not written with a reader, other than myself, in mind. My spontaneous syntax and jumbled flow purposefully haven't been edited out of existence (a difficult task!). I do not share these excerpts as examples of literature or to be an emotional exhibitionist, but to demonstrate the loose form a personal journal can take.

Some journals are organized with dreams, plans, daily events, and subpersonalities in neat, accessible categories. This can be useful. Ira Progoff (1975) has written on the subject of "journaling," and I recommend reading his *At a Journal Workshop* for in-depth discussion. My journal is like me, as yours will be like you. I mentally "change gears" very quickly and sometimes erratically. I learn primarily through my ears, and so my work sounds like me—at least to my ear it does! I am neither a timid nor genteel person, and so my journal is written in the broad terms that characterize my life. Because I wasn't posing for an audience, my warts and crudity are apparent.

Poetry—that spare, evocative mystery of language that moves us beyond common prose—is a particularly fine expressive tool. In journal poetry I have given myself permission to speak with intensity, economy, and emotion without the need to calculate the effect on a reader. The poetry in my journal was not written to share. It was written to express the essence of my feelings for the pure pleasure and relief of the process. I do not rhyme nor adhere to any technical rules. I just write what I feel, as cleanly as possible.

> *I had a back-bending bellyful*
> *Before he was born.*
> *How he thrashed and made himself known*
> *Months before he appeared!*
> *That time is a trace memory in my womb.*
>
> *I had a bellyful of dirty diapers,*
> *Broken sleep, teething, PTA*
> *Chicken pox on Christmas*
> *Though I've nearly forgotten it all.*
>
> *Now I've got a heartful of fire*
> *The coals burn my nipples and scorch my brain*
> *The heat chars my courage*
> *Blisters my hope, incinerates belief.*
> *This heartful is too much with me.*

When I write, I talk to Maggie. That's my journal's name—Maggie. Somehow she, like a best friend, is always ready to listen, accept my complaints, absolve my wickedness, and record my brags. She takes me as I am and comes back for more. I keep no secrets back and conceal no reprehensible ideas. With her, I am baldly honest, sloppily sentimental, foolishly grandiose, and remarkably funny. She passes no judgments on me that I didn't think of first, and she is totally devoted to me—what a pal, what a comfort and, strangely, what a teacher!

Maggie contains doodles, sketches, plans, and records of back sliding. When my life is intense, I use her frequently. I have carried her in my purse, ready to listen to a fleeting idea, record a friend's wisdom, or mark an occasion of pain. I usually put my dreams into her for later work and contemplation. I like summing up my day in her pages. Sometimes I let her gather dust for days and usually regret it as I try to recall who I was, day before yesterday.

She shows me, concretely, what my progress is, where I've fallen short, what my intensity was. This has been comforting to me. I discovered that I had most access to my anger and anxiety when I was premenstrual; that became a time of withdrawal from others and intense self-disclosure to Maggie. By studying Maggie, I learned how Patrick's Death Day Ritual (more about that later) evolved.

Maggie has listened longer than I could ever expect or hope another friend would tolerate my yammering "I, I, I." She is the history of my spiritual and practical evolution. Now she lives on computer disks. Previously, she's been a blank account book, a loose-leaf binder and three-by-five cards. Now she is a virtual folder. She's versatile and also fertile.

Thank you, Maggie.

Ritual Thirty-five: Journaling

I encourage—nay! exhort—you to keep a journal. It needn't be as elaborate as Progoff suggests, but certain things are profoundly useful to record. A journal is an intimate history, one written without an outside audience in mind. If you share yours with a therapist or a trusted ally, be certain you are not writing "for publication," because that is inhibiting.

I suggest you date every entry, make note of your mundane daily circumstances, and allow yourself to be entirely honest. My journal shows my hardness as well as my pliancy, my vulgarity as well as my refinement. A reader would find I am a "whole thing," not a person living a role written by convention. I make "to do" lists, paste in picture, draw charts, and press flowers in mine.

Women should record their place in their menstrual cycles and everyone should make daily note of their personal physical condition, both pleasant and challenging.

Speculation, conclusions, decisions, and humor have a place. Vital, I believe, are dreams and dream fragments because patterns may emerge. Once I had a series of apparently unrelated dreams that, on later examination, proved to all involve being insulted or disregarded. That discovery opened me to an important self-sabotage I was unwittingly committing.

I have found it useful to have a time set aside for my journal work. Evenings work well, just before bed, as I sort and empty onto the page impressions, events, and feelings. Sometime I plan or pledge or forgive. It clears my head wonderfully before rest.

You would do well to read Ira Progoff's book, *At a Journal Workshop: The Basic Text and Guide for Using the Intensive Journal Process*, or another book on the subject. There are many examples and exercises that I haven't room for here, but value greatly.

Auditory Drawing

Originally, I balked at the notion of drawing or painting. The mystery of putting pencil to paper and producing a likeness seemed outside my capacity. Because my hands appreciate the dimensionality and texture of clay, basketry, sewing, and cooking. I have not developed well in flat planes such as painting and drawing. I "don't get flat" is my flip way of saying there is mystery in how, in a few strokes, an artist can make a running wolf streak across a page or a reflection delight the eye from daubs of paint. Now, I look at drawing as an expressive process rather than a goal. I do not feel a need to draw a picture of something. A hard, jagged-edged scrawl expresses anger effectively; no need for a meticulous sketch. A puddle of yellow paint in the midst of feathered strokes of green may evoke spring; no need for carefully crafted daffodil portraits.

Auditory drawing is one way to evoke the images and emotions tied up in memory. By visualizing grief being discharged in the drawing process, I was able to recall and release stagnant energy tied up in visual memory. A friend described a scene he recalled when Patrick and I were together. With eyes closed and a large paper pad before me, I allowed myself to draw with a medium-width marker pen. As my intuitive side took over and I concentrated on the memory as described by my friend, I made many strokes on the paper with the sole purpose of expressing my feelings.

Ritual Thirty-six: Auditory Drawing

First, experiment with auditory drawing by working with your eyes closed while thinking of particular moments that you know are important for your grieving process. For me, key moments were those that stayed vividly alive in my senses and memory. Some were happy—receiving or giving a gift. Others poignant—hearing a familiar melody or tasting a once-shared treat. Some were visual—a pile of books beside a bed, and others were tactile—the feel of a silk pillow. All of these were instances of awareness that were loaded with significance. Keep your marker pen loosely grasped—don't over-control it—and make sweeping motions over the large pad of newsprint you use. Don't worry about boundaries or going off the page, it doesn't matter. A medium marker pen in the color of your choice is best, since it doesn't gouge the page nor lend itself to small, tightly controlled movements. Don't try to draw realistically the objects or faces in your memory unless you are already adept; rather, allow your intuitive processes to direct your hand. Breathe deeply and use a different page for each memory. You might play music that you shared with the person you've lost, or have a friend read a letter to or from the person, or tell stories about him or her. Do not talk during your auditory drawing sessions.

Dreams

The following discussion and journal examples represent my approach to working with dreams. Other therapists and theorists might differ with my understanding and procedures. Many approaches to dreams can be found. Avoid publications that give pat answers or formulas, which can be terribly misleading. Each of us creates our dreams from our recent experiences, deep memories, and mysterious forces from the unconscious. There is no one-size-fits-all interpretation code. There is nothing as individual and personal as a dream. My own views are shaped largely by the ideas of Carl Jung and Fritz Perls.

Dreams are shadow visitors emerging from hidden parts of ourselves. They are projections of our unconscious and hold potent meaning. Dreams are feelings, experiences, ideas, sagas, instructions, and threats that appear to us in sleep, when we are most vulnerable and when our ordinary waking reality is suspended. Some rare dreams appear to be prophetic or clairvoyant, offering suggestion of events yet to occur or happening at a great distance. These are outside the scope of this book.

Other dreams are problem-solving events. We go to sleep puzzled or blocked in our search for solutions and awaken with answers or seed ideas that can be developed productively. In a moment of madness, I once agreed to make six hundred sandwiches for a group to which I belonged. When the day of reckoning was approaching, I was in a near panic. A dream came to me of applying the egg salad and deviled ham to the bread with a clean paint roller. Desperately, I tried the idea, and it worked wonderfully well. Frivolous as this example may seem, it saved me from a dreary day, and it demonstrates the rich, creative possibilities of dream time.

Other dreams hold what Freud called "day residue." We spend a day cleaning the garage or dealing with mechanics about the car, then find ourselves continuing these routine activities in sleep. It well may be that these everyday experiences are being "processed" for storage in the unconscious. Such dreams may have little significance for expressive grief work. However, the possibility exists that they may emerge as metaphors. After all, cleaning the garage has us sorting through old things, some worthless, some of value. It could be something of importance to consider.

Some dreams are so garbled that we despair of understanding their significance, though experience has shown that they may be laden with valuable teachings. What is needed are tools to decipher their messages. The discussion that follows will demonstrate some of the most useful ways I have found for dealing with such strange dreams. This cannot be an exhaustive exploration, because of the complexity of the study. What I can offer is some beginning direction.

With certain dreams, we have a haunting and persistent feeling of importance. These dreams are numinous. We know they connect us with a power and wisdom beyond our own. We may call this power God, the collective unconscious, or something else, but we *know* that something of significance has visited us in sleep. Again, we need tools to understand.

It appears that the third of our lives we spend in sleep may be critical to our sanity. It is certainly an enduring mystery, fraught with importance. People deprived of the opportunity to dream (not just deprived of sleep) often show symptoms of impaired psychological functioning. They sometimes become delusional and hallucinate; judgment is impaired, and behavior is unpredictable. Perhaps we must process our daily lives in dreams and store the results in our unconscious to avoid being cluttered by unassimilated material that could make us act and feel crazy. Some cultures, such as the Native American Hopi, are guided by the dreams of the people, the teachings those dreams offer, and the ability to enter "Dream Time" to receive sacred instruction for waking life.

Even though some people claim they never dream, laboratory studies have established that nearly everyone dreams at frequent intervals during each night. People who claim that they do not dream are probably blocking recall. Drugs, alcohol, extreme fatigue, and certain brain disturbances can suppress the capacity to dream. The irrational waking behavior associated with these conditions may be partly the consequence of dream deprivation.

It is possible to train yourself to recall dreams. There is a never-never land between sleep and waking where we float half-in, half-out of consciousness. This state can be used to "plant" ideas in the unconscious by using the techniques of creative visualization and self-suggestion. Repeat over and over, as you fall asleep, "I will dream and remember tonight." Have your journal or other recording material nearby so you can record your dream as soon as you come into wakefulness. Persist. You will be touching on the most mysterious third of your life when you access your dreams.

For the grieving person, dreams are often vivid, frightening, evocative, and persistent. They may disrupt rest and haunt the waking hours. We know that some message is pounding on the gates of consciousness, and yet we are blocked from understanding. We will do well to heed these visitors from our depths, for they may release us from misery and point toward a productive pathway to growth.

It is the nature of dreams to be symbolic, even as they spring from reality. Dream images have a literal meaning—they are the boats and trains and planes we dream about—*and* they have a symbolic meaning. They also represent something else, such as a loved one's departure. In symbolism, one entity represents another. The flag is the symbol of the country; a wedding ring is a symbol of marriage; a dollar bill is a symbol of buying power. These ordinary symbols have consensual validation—that is, almost everyone agrees on their meaning.

There is no consensual validation on the meaning of dream symbols. Dreams cannot be properly deciphered through simplistic formulas based upon predetermined meanings for certain symbols. A black horse appearing in my dream might symbolize power and escape; in yours, it might mean misfortune and doom. Our unique personalities, experiences, and circumstances shape the personal meaning of the symbols that appear in our dreams.

No one else can interpret your dream; it is for you to decode. A skilled counselor or knowledgeable friend can offer perspective and guidance. Journal work and creative projection can be illuminating.

Courageously facing and learning from our dreams is one of the most effective ways to further our grief work and find direction for our lives. It is appropriate at every stage of life and in every emotional circumstance.

Earlier, I referred to Jung's concept of the "shadow" part of personality. The shadow is the powerful, dark aspect of who we are that holds all those characteristics we find unacceptable—violence, anger, vengefulness, immorality, slyness, deceit. Its messages to us are delivered directly from the unconscious and are laden with the seeds of creativity. But the aspects of the personality that are sheltered in the shadow, like my witch, can dominate our disposition and our decisions, albeit clandestinely. When we burst out with invective and rage, scarcely recognizing our own voices, our shadow is probably at the mike.

Once I threw a glass of cold water at a nasty child, something unthinkable when I am in my "right mind." This expression of my shadow was not my ordinary behavior. When we are weary or unguarded, as in grief, the shadow may shatter our reasonable, calm, and civilized way of doing business. Many women find their shadow bursting forth when they are premenstrual. This is an excellent time to work diligently to unlock the secrets of dreams, surprising impulses, and irrational feelings.

If we are to disarm the destructive parts of the shadow, thereby taking charge of our own energy, there is no better way than to begin to understand our dreams. It is in our dreams that the shadow stands, revealed and vulnerable to the good sense and determination of the conscious mind.

Dreams instruct and warn us against our own impulses and self-sabotage. They point the way to our unfinished business—unexpressed, unintegrated anger, fear, confusion, and grief. They may, of course, be happy and confirming. Significantly, therapists speak of "emptying out" a dream of its symbols. With a combination of free associations and creative projection, we convert the symbols to comprehensible messages.

Free association is one way to find the meaning behind dream symbols. What follows is a verbatim excerpt from my journal that illustrates free association. I had a dream in which a spider appeared. I was puzzled—what did the spider mean to me?

Spider: *creepy—sinister—scary—poisonous—fangs—husband-eater—Joe's—husband-death—fault—me—bad wife—destroyer—vengeful—unfair—not me—web-weaver—beautiful— graceful—strong—productive—protective—motherly—me—bad mother—dead child—dead husband—tangled web we weave—no deceit—not mine—theirs—Joe and Pat—dead heroes—dead victims—live victims—the kids—me—all wrapped up in misery—poisoned—trapped—pointless.*

Such stream-of-consciousness thinking, if allowed to flow verbally or on paper, can be immensely revealing, expressive, and cleansing. Any element of a dream may be used for free association. It is important to speak or write quickly without stopping to analyze, criticize, or explore. Whatever comes to mind is said or written. We must move beyond our rehearsals. By injecting the pressure to "Keep writing!" we give ourselves a useful structure. The time pressure also acts to suspend the critic that lives in each of us.

Dreams should be recorded immediately upon awakening. I keep a pad and felt-tip pen handy so I can grab a key image before the dream is lost to my waking consciousness. I write in considerable detail in order to have material for creative projection or free association. *Every element in a dream is a projection of self*, and they may all be explored. We can "become" a dust mop, an heiress, a sword, a bearded revolutionary, the sun, a sailboat, or a Mozart sonata. If something appears in our dream, it reflects who we are. Each element has vitality of its own, even small items may be highly significant. The scarier an element is, the more energy it contains. Therefore, decoding such dreams holds great promise of self-understanding.

The following is an edited excerpt from my journal. It is not directly related to my bereavement. I chose it because it demonstrates the decoding of a very cryptic dream. It shows my use of creative projection and free association. I began by noting the date, describing the dream, and commenting upon my feelings on awakening. I also made sure to note my main activities during the previous day, feelings I had about coworkers and a client, and my place in my menstrual cycle. *The dream was recorded first, the detail added later.* Note that most of this material is written in the first person ("I, me, mine"), in the present tense and with the active voice—"I am." This is a convention that I use for recording dreams. It feels more real and "here-and-now," which is important in expressive work. I clearly was not writing for an audience. I hope the language does not give offense.

June 9: *Wednesday, three days after my period. Worked at Day Care Center/DS is a consummate jerk/DH has mental hemorrhoids/FI getting better—she laughed today!*

Dream: *I am on a tropical beach all alone. It's a picture postcard of paradise. I am dressed for work—pantyhose, heels, makeup—the works. There are no footprints on the sand except my own, and they are from these idiotic shoes I'm wearing. The heels make little wells in the sand where the sea water comes up. I look back and see a progression of little wells following me. I see something climb out of first one, then another, then all the wells—lots of things—sort of like something between a slug, an ant, and a spider. Big, slimy, muscular things—they all grow or swell quickly to the size of a hen. They are everywhere behind me. Ahead the beach still looks like a "Visit Bermuda" poster.*

I'm running faster and faster, leaving more and more holes behind me, from which come more and more of these horrible creatures. They don't seem interested in me, but I'm terrified that they'll want to eat me or something. I'm really afraid.

Suddenly I'm flying—I'm in a flock of Canadian geese, all honking at once. It's a wonderful sound with the wind in my ears and the whoosh of their huge wings soaring through the sky. I wonder how it is I'm with them and then discover that I'm a goose! Just as I realize this, I see hunters in a ditch and I scream.

Woke up feeling interrupted—as if the dream had more to show me—glad to be awake. Desperate to warn the others—like there's something I have to do—lives depend on me sounding the warning. I'm scared, then disgusted, thinking of those creatures. What in hell do the high heels have to do with anything? Pantyhose? I heard a guy hung himself with his unfaithful girlfriend's pantyhose. That's the worst pantyhose story I know. Then there was the guy who got his wristwatch band caught in the crotch of—no, I'm getting silly—avoiding this dream. It (I) feels significant.

Will do a few CP's [creative projections] *to see what's what:*

I'm the hunter. I'm crouched in a cold pond, I've got my shotgun and ammunition, and I'm waiting in ambush for the geese. I like to kill birds. It feels good when I follow them with my barrel and then, leading a little, squeeze off a blast. If I do it right, the bird and the shot get to the same place at the same time. Then that big bird just tumbles out of the sky like a bag of laundry down the cellar stairs. Yes, I'm a sportsman. I'm death hidden in the rushes, holding a double-barreled shotgun, watching beautiful, free birds in my gun sight.

I'm a Canadian goose flying, one of many—it would be hard to tell us apart until attention is paid to our voices. I look like all the other geese, but my voice is different. We all have different voices—I don't sound like anyone else! Flying over a beautiful autumn countryside, there is a pond with room enough for our flock, and the one down there near the rushes is calling to us. I'm big and strong—I can beat my wings for hours, days, weeks. I'm strong and unique.

This idea was a revelation to me, and I went on at length about my uniqueness. The symbol of the bird was clear—I was a unique being, even though I looked pretty undistinguished. I was part of a large flock, and we were all vulnerable to any blood-thirsty sociopath with a gun getting out his sexual jollies or armed aggression by killing something free and beautiful.

I went on with feelings about my husband and son being wild geese too, singing special songs as they passed along. The same hunter, Clinical Depression, got them both. I reached other conclusions, but this gives an indication of the value of creative projection, at least to me.

Sometimes I find it enlightening to have two parts of my dream dialogue with each other—it's a no-holds-barred confrontation when I do. More often than not, the dream elements are antagonistic to each other at first. I "went back into" my dream to empty out the meaning of the high heels and the beach.

High Heels: I'm having a hard time doing my job. You're too mushy, Beach; I can't walk on you.

Beach: You're making ugly marks on me, letting horrible stuff out. You hurt me. You disfigure me. Go back to the city where you belong—only bare feet should touch me. I'm Eden: unsullied, unexplained. You don't belong here.

High Heels: I wasn't meant for this! I was meant for smooth streets, carpeted rooms, elevators. If you were a ballroom, I'd be happy.

Beach: Meanwhile, you mess me up. I was beautiful, peaceful, idyllic before you came galumping and marring me.

High Heels: If I can't use you, you're worthless.

Beach: Typical! Unless something is of immediate utility to you, you think it's worthless. You're silly—a twisted, self-defeating artifice, more an inhibition than useful. You're a monument to vanity. Leave me alone—you hurt me. I was natural, whole, and graceful until you showed up. You're a show-off.

High Heels: I make Peg's legs look long and slim. Is that so bad?

Beach: And torture her anatomy. Now look at me! Ant-slug-spiders crawling out of their dens, ruining my peace all because you, you phony, stabbed me.

High Heels: I didn't put the uglies in you, Beach, I just let them out.

Here I discovered that there was a conflict between my vanity, symbolized by the shoes, and the natural part of myself, symbolized by the beach. Later I explored the uglies and found out painful but important truths about myself. All elements in a dream can be used for free association or creative projection.

These demonstrations are pastel in comparison with the vivid experience of engaging in dream work with a skilled therapist. Much of my most significant work was done with my therapist's guidance; a set of objective ears is very helpful. The journal is a refuge and the right place to keep your dream records, whether you decode them alone or with help.

Reframing

Another tool for expanding our awareness and shaping our responses is reframing. Reframing is illustrated by the optimist who sees the glass as half full or the pessimist who sees the hole rather than the doughnut. One of the psychotherapist's most powerful devices when a client feels trapped and hopeless is to reframe the situation to highlight opportunities and foster empowerment. Like moving beyond a restrictive or outdated viewpoint, reframing breaks us out of narrow and self-limiting ways of thinking and into a world of new possibilities. It serves particularly well when we are in crisis.

Reframing is not denial of pain or anger; it is not a "Pollyanna" attitude, nor is it wall-papering over the cockroaches. It is, rather, a technique for viewing adversity that creates an alchemical change of energy—from despair to hope. It means seeking the best possible interpretation, searching each difficult situation for what it has to teach, and exploring the range of conceivable options. Some people seem to do this intuitively; for others, it is a learned skill.

Joan Borysenko (1988) says, "Using the energy that is tied up in resistance but channeling it in a new direction is the mental equivalent of the martial arts, where subtle shifts in balance allow the opponent's energy to be used to your own advantage. In reframing, the opponent is often your own mind-set" (p. 141).

You will recall the Bennetts and the crisis presented by Dan's terminal illness. Rose, Sylvia's mother, and the senior Bennetts were emotionally and intellectually inflexible, holding on to their initial responses to the dreadful news of Dan's impending death. They were apparently unable to progress beyond their initial devastation. Rose's characteristic and conditioned pattern of bewailing fate, rather than demanding lessons from it, served her poorly. The elder Bennetts held to a rigid belief system that did not allow them to accommodate wisely to conditions they found intolerable. That Dan did not share their vision of salvation, that God had chosen to take their son unseasonably, and that nothing had prepared them to open to new ideas, were concepts they faced with habitual mind-sets serving to isolate them. Sadly, they froze into emotionally and intellectually rigid patterns just when the options were closing and when Dan had an urgent need for validation and intimacy.

The Bennett family (and I) were in a constant process of reframing our experiences throughout the intense period of Dan's dying. As he explained, "When I first got sick and found out how bad it was, my reaction was to be pissed off. There was so much, that I wanted to do, I felt like I'd been tripped by a piano wire . . . I'd stumbled and fallen. I was really sorry for myself, sorry for Sylvia, sorry for the boys, sorry, sorry, sorry. So much has happened since, that I'm sort of eager, to tell the truth, for what comes next. Not that I'd turn down a cure or remission!"

He compressed a lifetime of changes into four months. Necessity, in his case, was the mother of innovative reframing. Dan's transitions from matter-of-fact arrangements, through bitter anger, to serene acceptance of his impending death allowed him a dignified and sensitive passage from this life.

Sylvia moved from intense anger at Dan's refusal of heroic medical intervention, to anger at the world for going on without him, to anger at God's merciless (it seemed at first) testing of the family, to a quality of acceptance that was neither resigned nor bitter. In the course of her growth, she found what was important to her: love and intimacy. In crystallizing her core values, she found an unexpected, unique purpose for her own life. She took longer than Dan to move from anguish to understanding, but then she had more time. She summed it up in a poem.

> *Black dog snarling in the shadows*
> *Name him Despair.*
> *Black dog fetching sticks*
> *Call him Hope.*
> *Which dog will I feed?*

Today, Sylvia works as a pediatric nurse-practitioner and helps train volunteers for her local hospice. She speaks poignantly of the needs of the dying in terms of Dan's determined and dignified autonomy. She talks, too, of the creative possibilities of rituals for the bereaved. She has remarried, something she swore she'd never do; the pain of another loss had at one time seemed too great to risk. Brandon, the pediatrician she married, is vigorous and supportive. She says she cherishes every hour of their time together. Sylvia's life shows that creative growth is possible in passing through grief's fiery furnace.

Mike moved dramatically from his initial withdrawal and resentment to eventually approaching Dan for guidance. His reframing came hard; it took his father's heartfelt, skilled sharing and visible personal changes to open the way for him. Adolescence is a time of internal turmoil, irresolution, and questioning; when the exterior landmarks are disrupted, the youth feels the reverberation internally. Dan understood this, and he directed a great deal of his effort to leaving a record that would support Mike in growing through the breach caused by his own death. Without Dan's foresight, Mike was in danger of feeling abandoned and unworthy, perhaps guilty, and certainly confused. In real ways, his life hung in balance until he reframed his misery to creative ends. Today, Mike is a sports journalist featured in prestigious publications and, not accidentally, a competitive sailor of America's Cup status. He still rides for recreation and is married. He has two boys. The firstborn is Daniel McKenzie Bennett.

Teddy, the youngest, is now nearly a man himself, though still living at home. He looks like a young Dan. His memory of his father is filmy, not quite reliable, but he cherishes the complete record of Dan's passage in which he, Teddy, was a significant player. Dan's last gift was a carved rosewood bear; this is on Teddy's altar. His work has been more in the nature of constructing a vision of the father he barely remembers; it is a good one. He had no difficulty accepting Brandon as stepdad. A picture of Dan, grinning from the deck of the *Good Times*, is prominent on his wall.

For me, the lessons of this experience were many: I enhanced my ability to value and encourage full expression, even of unlovely thoughts and feelings, and to believe in the transmutation of energy. Until the shadow is acknowledged, the conversion of its energy is slow and difficult. I no longer doubt human capacity to adapt, learn, and transcend.

The prime teachings are to put the best possible interpretation on events, behavior, and people, as well as to search diligently for the lessons implicit in even the most devastating experiences. This does not imply that all questions can be answered or that pain is welcomed. This mind-set has served me well personally and professionally—and it is a good example of reframing.

The person who customarily finds gloom in change, challenge, or loss of control is, in many ways, disabled. Often this way of structuring experience is an attempt to avoid disappointment or disillusion; the cost is living in perpetual darkness, hopelessly. The person may, earlier in life, have been wounded so sharply that all creative energy had to be marshaled simply to stay alive. Changing habitual negative patterns of thought and response takes work that is best learned in times of strength. The reward is parallel to that of the person who eats wholesomely, exercises regularly, laughs often, and sleeps deeply. Physical sickness comes less frequently and, when it does, is met with ready resources. When one has learned to habitually reframe potentially destructive experiences, the mechanisms are in place to grow through, rather than be crushed by, the losses in life.

To reframe is work requiring consciousness, will, and practice. The decision to change the internal focus involves consciousness of how and to which stresses one typically responds, an unblinking look at assumptions about hope, the comprehension of myths that govern life choices, and knowledge about characteristic ways of reacting. It also requires the will to modify and to expand beyond ordinary limits of behavior. This process takes practice, since old habits yield reluctantly and new ones are born of repetition. To view life's tests differently is a decision.

Watch for the indicators—truth buttons—that reveal your way of reacting to stress. Some people tell themselves scary stories, mining events for every possible disaster. Others act tough or accepting without expressing their feelings, thereby internalizing or denying their misery. I have a tendency to "refer" my stress to my spine, stiffening it and being "brave." I carry on. Most people have similar physical responses, characteristic ways of reflecting emotional disarray. When these are known, consciousness is present and becomes the signal for change. Without denying unhappiness, one can express and empty it. This awareness is the first step of reframing, far from "making nice" or "putting on a good face." Mantras, affirmations, visualizations, rituals, dream work, journaling, and movement now have practical applications. It is a time to use intellect, to search the landscape for all the views possible. One perception is not enough; creative thought is needed. What is the best possible interpretation of the event? Consider the players; consider the circumstances; consider the potential. Be kind (to yourself, most of all), be fanciful, if necessary, but crank consciousness from its rut and break new ground.

When the will to change is present, a backup plan—devised in a calm time—can be a powerful ally. It is often difficult to be creative, to pull out of doldrums, when overwhelmed with stress. By planning a strategy for the inevitable hard times of life, one is prepared. The backup plan supports hope. It highlights resources and opportunities that may not be as visible in difficult circumstances. It is an exercise in reframing. Establishing a viable back up plan is seldom obvious or easy. That which awaits discovery is rarely anticipated. It must be sought as diligently as a diamond miner who burrows through tons of rubble for the single precious gem.

Recall how Sylvia came to awareness that "things are as they should be" during her vision quest, despite the pain, anger, and impotence she first felt. Sylvia's poem is worth repeating here, as an example of the possibilities implicit in unsolicited sorrow.

> *There is mercy in a drenching rain*
> *Washing the dust and dog crap away,*
> *Leaving trees and city freshly cleansed.*
> *There is mercy in a raging storm*
> *Ravaging the coast and removing all*
> *The sailors' wine bottles and Twinkie wrappers.*
> *There is mercy in the ripping, rending pain*
> *In the agony of separation and unanswerable questions*
> *Removing all the etiquette, false smiles and*
> *Untried, politic assumptions about reality,*
> *Leaving truth and love and laughter and God in its wake.*

To successfully reframe rending pain, as Sylvia so poignantly demonstrates, requires energy, determination, and practice. The alchemical change from common grief to precious creativity is accomplished not magically or mystically, but through tenacious effort.

Ritual Thirty-seven: Reframing

As you do this ritual, remember this point: Put the best possible interpretation, consistent with reality, on the event. There is no way to honestly reframe a fire that destroys a home, along with all the practical and treasured things it contained, so that the event is the equivalent of a picnic in the park.

What you are after is putting the best possible interpretation and, by extension, the most hopeful, pleasurable projection on the aftermath.

1. If you've let ritual 1 slide, refresh yourself with it now.

2. From the following list of hurtful situations choose two or three to reframe, remembering to put the best possible interpretation on the situation that is possible given the personnel, the impact, and your hopeful vision.

   Example: Sprained ankle. This means that the obligation to do errands and be very active is not practical for a few days. I'll improvise the best I can, let go of the aggravation and use the time to read a couple of books and catch up on my correspondence.

   ____ A job loss

   ____ A non-injury car accident

   ____ Someone not acknowledging a gift

   ____ The cat having an unexpected pregnancy and delivery

   ____ Losing your wallet

   ____ Unseasonable rainstorm

   ____ Tickets being sold out at an event you wanted to attend

   ____ Computer meltdown

   ____ A friend not inviting you to a party

   ____ A series of phone calls with hang-ups

   ____ Discovering dry rot in the porch joist

   ____ Having a horde of shirttail relatives arriving on the weekend your bowling team may be in the finals

   ____ A week of dramatically bad weather predicted

It probably seems like a long trail we've traveled together. We've touched in on many principles and practices. If we've worked well together, you have a collection of tools and insights to carry forward into the next challenging chapter, one for which we have been preparing. Don't falter now—rather, affirm your initial contract to heal and experience the rebirth of pleasure. Life is happening, right now.

CHAPTER 8

Rituals of Goodbye

Goodnight, ensured release,
Imperishable peace,
Have these for yours.

—A. E. Housman

In this book I have presented several core ideas: sorrow is a universal experience; hope is essential to a vital life; pleasure is possible—even probable; and the alchemy of suffering may produce a precious change of consciousness. None of these are simple. All can be observed when attention is properly directed..

Sorrow is complex and is felt in degrees or increments. There is sorrow when the last child graduates from high school, for it means at least two separations. It signals that childhood is over and that our parental role is significantly changed. There is sorrow at the collapse of any relationship whether marriage, friendship, or collegial. There is sorrow when health fails and the time of easy vigor closes. The loss of illusion is painful as is the loss of status, time of life, or place. Grief is the deepest, most profound and life-altering increment in the "sorrow scale."

I wish you well in your efforts, for they are worthy of your best energy. Imagine my hand held out, beckoning. Between us is a wasteland of thistles, nettles, and sinkholes. I am pointing to a safe path over to where I am now standing, beside a summer river on a luminous day. It is good to be here, and I invite you to make the trip and experience the rare and simple pleasures of life once again. All that has gone before is preparation. We are at the critical juncture.

"Goodbye." How we pull back from the word, the reality! It signals an ending, the completion of a phase or cycle of life. Funerals, memorial services, monuments, grave markers, and condolence cards all point the way; yet most often the crucial word is left unspoken. We avoid finality. And, in avoiding it, we block our alchemical changes and hobble our progress through our grief process. It is terribly hard to "go on alone," yet if we do not somehow make the break with our illusions, time of life, place, or loved one, then we are crippled in life without retrieving or reviving what has passed. We make a bleak testimony with our devotion. When we have moved through the fire and can feel pleasure again, energy flows. We are able to plan usefully to take the experience into the world, wholesomely.

How can we bear the pain of admitting that we are at the terminating point? We must first understand the purpose of "goodbye" to reconcile ourselves to this final movement through our grief process. The use of ritual is particularly valuable in this context. Ritual is not only useful in recruiting support, but in making real the passage of time and energy. The form of the ritual must be in harmony with the belief system, emotional vitality, and spiritual vision of the mourner. It often seems as we approach the critical moment of release, we almost say the word—*goodbye*—and then retreat with our work unfinished.

I was afraid I'd forget or be disloyal to Joe and Patrick, not understanding at first that to say goodbye is not to develop amnesia. Just as I can wave "so long" from an airport terminal to departing friends without forgetting them, so is it possible to break the bond with the one who has died without losing the memory of the closeness of the relationship. Its importance in our life is not lost to fond memory. The influence of such loving ways always belongs to us.

We must affirm that the life coursing through us has purpose beyond sorrow. The alchemical changes possible in the grief process will imbue the events with meaning and confirm the preciousness of our own lives. We may become less profligate with our assets and more joyful in our experiences, difficult as it is to believe in the beginning.

I was not a church member when Patrick died, and I felt confusion as to what I should do. He had chosen to die in Carmel, California, by carbon monoxide poisoning in his car. I lived 500 miles away, in San Diego. I was at a stage in my life when I found traditional religious rites hollow. The following excerpts from my journal may seem harsh to those who have found comfort in conventional forms of funeral arrangements. I recognize and respect that each of us must find peace and meaning in our own characteristic style. I offer these journal excerpts as windows on my own evolution with the hope that they will provide you with useful glimpses as you manage yours. Do not take them as exhortations to stand in the same unevolved place I was as they were written. Take them as one woman's starting point. I am much altered since their writing as the rest of this book demonstrates. Stan, Katie, and Peter are my other children.

I am afraid to examine the depths of my pain. . . . I am going to venture in a little further. Son-boy-man. I love you. You are memories and intellectual understanding. Phantom, not a healthy man. I won't hear any more stories about Russian countesses who speak of things as "giftedly drawn" or "splish-splash" being the sound of dripping water. Your dialect was magnificent. Your sense of the absurd and your kindness in characterizing others delights me. I remember doing dishes with you when you were small, and we did intellectual games, "name five mountain ranges beginning with 'A.'" You named seven. I remember your agony at baseball season when you were humiliated by sadistic coaches and savage classmates for your inability to hit the ball. I remember your only fight, when you got even with the guy who punched your typhoid shot. I remember you in a coat of Brillo mail as the lead in a school play—"The Mouse That Roared"—you were so handsome!

I could fill pages with memories. And I want your hug. Son, son—I am weeping now—can't see the pages. I know you're gone. I don't want you gone. I don't know how many children I have—three or four? Three living—one dead. What does my eldest son do? Float as ash on the sea or make surfboards? Answer me, damn it, Pat! What limbo is this? You are, you aren't, you are. I could tear you out of me . . . I am strong enough, and I know this writing loosens our bonds. I don't want you gone. I cannot (read: will not) do the clean and beautiful thing Stan and Peter and Bulldog [a buddy] *did.*

Good ol' Bulldog—strong, virile, handsome, fighting hard to be a little kid and manhood coming on fast. He reminds me of a Scots chieftain with humor. Bulldog went with Peter and Stan the night we learned of your death—your self-murder. They went surfing. The sea is a mighty ally to those wanting a fight and communion and competence and a sense of their own vitality.

And they went to Carmel. On a mountain all green like the Ireland you loved so much—with fingers of fog miles below—clear icy water hitting hard the shore. In a field of grasses, rocks, and wild flowers they built you a cairn. Not the confining man-sized grave of ordinary men. No. A huge statement in letters eight feet high of hauled stone: "TO PAT. SUBLEJOS." Sublejos—a secret word. They put daisies in the hollows of the P and A of your name. In the picture that good Bulldog took, Peter is joyfully holding his dog, the wind ruffling his straw-blond hair, and an innocent smile on his sixteen-year-old face. The pictures are real and clear. I love my sons and Bulldog.

And I want Patrick to stride through the door, accuse me in his inimitable way of sentimentality and melodrama. God how I felt his contempt for my storms and changes—how afraid I was of his evaluation . . .

Patrick is dead. Patrick Joseph-Elliott Pleskunas, twenty-three, Yale graduate, linguist, artist, teacher, writer, humorist, observer, is dead. His body, not even fit for organ donation, is ash on the sea. I resisted the memorializers, the ritualizers, the conventionalists, and did not have a "service." He would approve. I hate dead bodies propped up in satin coffins, wearing eyeglasses while sanctimonious people carry on with their minicatharsis, their mindless incantations, their pious sentiments that boil down to "Thank God it's not me." Not yet, it isn't. I feel superior. I feel honest and nauseated at traditional cant.

The ideas and sentiments reflected in this journal entry are as foreign to me now as if they'd been written by a stranger. There is a curious blend of denial (if I don't have a service, he can't be dead), defiance ("I feel superior"), honesty, smugness, self-indulgence, and struggle. It is an awkward and valuable record of who I once was.

In the intervening years, I have come to respect funeral ritual and ceremony as serving two vital purposes—closure and memorial. I went on for months, torn between the hard-edged reality of Patrick's death and an irrational unwillingness to acknowledge it *emotionally*. Intellectually, I did all right. Closure came much later for me. Though my journal remains my memorial of my son, a more clearly ritualized and purposeful remembrance has grown from my later understanding of the need for wholesome acknowledgment of his central importance in my life.

Dropping handfuls of dirt on a coffin resting in a grave has a terrible finality. Those of us participating will return to our warm, fragrant, noisy houses, eat meals, watch the seasons pass, buy clothes, take trips, laugh, and welcome new children into the world, while our loved one will rest in the grave, senses extinguished, communicating nothing, and no longer participating in our lives. The wrench of separation is a rending of spirit and an agony beyond language. The wound, though, is clean. We can heal, given the right disposition, determination, and opportunity to do our grief work.

I now feel the wound of Patrick's death as clean, dry scar tissue. When I stretch it, as I am in this writing, or when I work with bereaved clients, I can feel the place on my psyche where I took the wound. In some ways, writing this piece hurts. But I am not obsessed—I do not think of Patrick hourly or even weekly. As I write, it has been twenty-eight years since his death, thirty-two since his father's. I am all right. By following my instincts and the teaching of wise healers, I have found my way through the same refining alchemical fire many people experience as part of their growth. I have closure at last on the misery. I do not want closure on the good parts of being Patrick's mother or Joe's wife. It is through ritual that I am able to have memorial and release.

There are four stages associated with the final phase of transmuting grief to creativity in expressive grief work: First, we express the resentment and anger associated with the loss. I have discussed this at considerable length. Second, we dredge our memories and recall the person we've lost and our associations about the person. Making a long list of "I remembers" is very useful and often primes the pump for the last two stages. Third, we do well to express our appreciations. Speaking or listing these brings balance and gives a sense of legacy from our absent loved one. Finally, and with much resolution, we give a benediction and say goodbye. These will be our rituals for this chapter. Courage!

Saying goodbye has always been hard for me. I don't like to see a carload of friends pull away. I don't like lingering admonitions at airports or giving kisses on the forehead in hospitals. Yet goodbye is as inevitable in life as hello. When I had advanced in my grief work sufficiently, it became clear to my therapist and me that the time had come to say goodbye. I resisted, but eventually the inevitability was unavoidable.

We made a ritual of me recounting my good memories of Patrick from his conception to his death. It took a long, long time, and I felt spiritual power supporting the painful effort. Visualizing him in a chair before me, I told Patrick how much I had appreciated him—how glad I was he had been born to me. I spoke of my sadness and confusion, but my anger was spent. As I spoke, I saw him fade before me—becoming less and less substantial. I wept to lose his red-gold thatch of hair, bright blue eyes, and rueful expression. I told him so. Still I permitted him to fade. At last, prompted by my friend-therapist, I said the momentous words:

> *Goodbye, Son. Goodbye, Patrick Joseph. Be good. I have to go on without you. Goodbye. I love you and will always love you—you will always be a source of pride. My heart hurts. I wish you well, whereever you go—goodbye. Goodbye. Goodbye. Go with my blessing, Son—goodbye.*

No words ever came harder or meant more. I had reached the final stage of grief—acceptance. I was facing an empty chair and a life with unknown potential. I was ready to live—I was nearly free of the fire. It only licks around my heels some now, mostly around anniversaries, which is why I have devised both a birth-day and a death-day anniversary ritual.

My rituals are short, changeable, and informal. Other people are more elaborate and ceremonial in their observations. For rituals to be meaningful, they must reflect the personality and needs of the people performing them. The marriage ritual of the Bantu tribal people of southern Africa would not meet the needs nor match the personalities of Portland Presbyterians. Both, evolving out of vastly different cultures and beliefs, are authentic and beautiful, and both satisfy the human need to celebrate the coming-together of a man and woman.

It would be atypical of me to forget significant dates. I suppose I will always remember Patrick's birth and death dates and others from his growing up. Rather than repress these times, I have chosen to honor them and make a small ritual that satisfies a primitive need within me.

Patrick's death day, February 27, comes in a dark time of the year. I go by myself to a secluded place and light a big, fat, red candle like he gave me for the last Christmas he lived. I remember "last" things—the last time I saw him, the last phone call, the last hug, the last letter. I weep. I sing "Let It Be" to the flickering flame, and I speak aloud of my love. This year I will add toning, which I have recently come to value, to my ritual. I will make the wordless sounds that reflect my love, regret, hope. Because I now live far from our old family home, I cannot go out and touch the bark of the loquat tree he planted. I cannot physically visit Sunset Cliffs, where we walked and talked. I cannot gather his brothers and sister close around me and exult in their vitality. What I *can* do is visualize all this, letting the healing energy of positive remembrance flow through me. When I feel complete, I say goodbye again and blow out the candle.

December 22, 1948 was his birthday. The winter solstice—shortest day of the year. I was nineteen. He was born at home, on a gray studio couch, delivered by a ruined old doctor who had sacrificed himself during the Second World War, but that's another story. Joe, his father, was twenty-one. He was there, though I can remember no comfort; instead of sweet-voiced encouragement to breathe, I got ether dripped on a gauze cone by a faceless nurse whom Dr. Eby had brought with him. I tried to be brave, like Melanie in *Gone With the Wind*. God! How young I was! How long ago! The very next December 21, Katie was born. Two untwinned babies in one year—how efficient of me!

One of my proudest motherly boasts is that neither of my Christmas-week children ever did without a birthday party or celebration. I was determined that "their" day (it alternated between the twenty-first and twenty-second on different years) be special for them.

It is my good fortune to have a precious friend, David Feinstein, who was also born on December 22—just two years before Patrick. I use the shining example of his maturation and goodness for hope; it's as if he is the living recipient and giver of the love I associate with that day. This is not to divide Katie out of my affection—she still has December 21 all to herself in my heart. David's sharing of birthdays with Patrick gives me a focus for my remembrance ritual for my son. I do not use David on this day nor any day as surrogate for Patrick, but as a friend who shares a memory. He has been a transcendent gift into my life, and his birthday proves it.

I make every effort to call David on their birthday and tell him how much I love him. I tell him some of the good events of the day and past year. I feel a summing up and marking of progress. We joke and share the emerging issues in our lives. The trust between us is total—we do not pull back from hard truths or bitter choices. Mostly, we take stock of the year with a positive emphasis. After the call, I go out into the forest. Though I seldom walked in the woods with Patrick, the times I did were memorable. I spend the time going through the happy moments of his life. I rarely weep. I give thanks that he lived, that he had successes, pleasures, loves, and appreciation. I assure myself that his short life was meaningful, that he is remembered positively. This book is part of his memorial, making something that may be useful to others out of the unwanted experience of his death.

A few years ago I began, at last, to give his things away. I had many boxes of old books, textbooks and art books, mostly. I had ceramic pieces he made and other precious things. It seemed time to give Katie, Stan, and Peter part of this legacy. I did it with a sense of ritual, honoring my son and his brief life. A birthday is meant to be happy, and I propose to keep it that way. Patrick will always be twenty-three—he will not change. I will remember the fat legs he had as a toddler, the practical jokes of his grade-school years, his singing "God Rest Ye Merry Gentlemen" outside the Unicorn Theater in San Diego, where he had treated us all to *The Wizard of Oz*. When I come in from the forest, I feel satisfied that he still has a special day set aside for pleasure and marking growth. And I have planted a candle-red rhododendron at my new home in his memory. Beneath it are buried his books, feeding the roots in the slow combustion of composting.

Because ritual making is a deep, intuitive human impulse, it can be channeled to support expressive grief work, to give memorial and bring closure. It is a living link with the good energy for the dear departed. The following five rituals are designed for addressing the deepest sorrow, grief at bereavement. Each is also applicable, with modification, to other losses. Please do not skip them because your loss was a pet, a place, a time of life, or something else hurtful—we know that not all grief flows from a person's death. Give yourself a wholesome ritual of remembrance—you will feel confirmed in the value of life. Courage! Go forward, Pilgrim. Discover your strengths and open to a fresh perspective on life.

Ritual Forty: Resentments and Regrets

It may seem strange to write and speak of resentments when you are grieving the goodness gone from your life, but we do resent the loss: this is natural. You may well have regrets about careless or unspoken words. There may have been actions between the dead and yourself that were regrettable. Remember the person who has died was human and as prone to mistakes of judgment and behavior as any of us. By expressing the feelings you have about your own actions or the other person's, you consciously release them, freeing both of you.

In your journal, with a trusted, courageous friend who will not stifle or be shocked at your passion or with your therapist, do the following three activities. Remember, you are emptying this stuff out, to be free of its toxic influence.

1. Do ritual 1. Breathe out *resentment* or *regret*, breathe in *acceptance.*

2. Using the person's name, begin *many* sentences with the following phrase: (Name), *I resent*—then let yourself express what has been left undone, what was hurtful, what the loss has meant in your life. Do not put effort into "being fair" or explaining away what you feel. Express it! Dump it out and be done with it to make room for what is worth cherishing.

   Example: Joe, I resent—bitterly and implacably—your dying as you did and leaving your body to be found by our son.

   Joe, I resent your silence and hoarding of feelings, never giving me a chance to help you find balance or to prepare myself.

3. Following the same steps as above express your regrets.

   Example: Joe, I regret I lost sympathy for you in your depression.

   Example: Joe, I regret not having a last chance to tell you how many ways I appreciate your life.

Ritual Forty-one: Appreciation

When you are not cluttered with regrets and resentments, there is energy freed to experience with appreciation the treasures of the relationship. While this is a poignant and deeply felt experience, it is also heartwarming and reassuring that the time spent together was worthwhile.

1. Do ritual 1. Breathe out *confusion*, breathe in *clarity.*

2. Following the pattern of ritual 40, recount the multitude of appreciations you have for the time you spent with the loved one. Do many!

Example: Joe, I appreciate that you did the best you could.

Example: Joe, I appreciate the children we created together.

Example: Joe, I appreciate the beauty of your body.

Ritual Forty-two: Remembering and Learning

When you have an important relationship, experiences are accumulated in memory. Learning, if you've been fortunate, is accrued. Some memories are profound, intimate, and mark major changes in life direction. Some learning may be so important that your whole world view is altered. These experiences are worthy of ritual.

1. Do ritual 1. Breathe out *sorrow*, breathe in *acceptance.*

2. Following the pattern of the previous two rituals, begin to address both what you have learned and those things you vividly remember from your relationship.

   Example: Joe, I remember being so very young and setting up our first home together.

   Example: Joe, I learned how to appreciate science from you, and I'm grateful.

Ritual Forty-three: Goodbye

I stand here, by the summer river, welcoming you to the rest of your life, when you have fully experienced the release of what is past and are open to what will be. It has been an arduous journey, and you have my admiration for having come so far. Gather your strength, lift your head, and commit to this important ritual. Wherever you are, know there is validating energy supporting you. Blessings on your courage and determination.

1. Do ritual 1. Breathe out *anguish*, breathe in *acceptance.*

2. Find a picture of the person lost to your life. Set it up so you are looking directly at it. If it isn't handy to use a picture, either put some object (coat, art piece, whatever) you strongly associate with the person or, better, maybe, visualize them in a chair across from you. Take time to see the set of the shoulders, characteristic expression, other intimate details. Breathe. Take long looks and, if tears come, allow yourself their cleansing help.

3. Compose yourself and say whatever last words you want to him or her. Sometimes the words come more easily if you use the format in the following example.

   Example: Joe, I want you to know that your existence shaped me, and I'm grateful.

   Example: Joe, I want you to know that I will dedicate my life to supporting creativity, expression, and intimacy in others as a result of my experiences with you.

   Example: Joe, I want you to know I recognize that you suffered, and that I was not the cause of it.

4. It is time to affirm your intention to live and your hopeful vision for your life.

   Example: Joe, I would have spent the rest of my life with you, but you chose differently. This has caused suffering for me and the children in a way that cannot be undone. I do not choose to spend my life in anguish, and today—right now—I declare my intention to be authentic, creative, and engaged. I choose life, that and nothing else for as many years as are granted to me. I am transcending suffering, and I have a glimpse of spiritual power that I will follow. I have already laughed a few times and expect—no! intend!—to do a whole lot more. I will not forget you, but I will not spend my life in mourning, either. I don't think you'd want that. I will love and enjoy our children. Alone, I will treasure our unborn grandchildren. Joe, your choice is not my choice. I choose life.

5. Here, my friend, we stand together, prepared to release the person you love to the Transcendent, or God, or whatever brings you comfort and understanding. I know the difficulty and the value. Please do it strongly and truthfully, *believe* what you are doing is proper, wholesome, and worthy. There are fateful, inevitable words to be said. Give whatever blessing you choose, make a pact with the future, and repeatedly say the word *goodbye*. **Let you feelings flow!**

   Example: Well, Joe, I stood on a lot of piers watching your submarine pull away and head for deep water. Here I am again. I wish you a good voyage with a good port and all the fresh cherries you can eat. I am going to turn around and go back to my new life. I am going back to college for my master's and I'm going to be the best mom on the block. I'm sure we'll miss you a lot for a while, but I intend to fill my life with good things in which you won't participate or even have approved of.
   Like I said, have a good trip. Travel light. I don't like to say it—I've never liked to say it, but goodbye. Goodbye. This hurts, but I am healing. Goodbye, Joe—husband, man, father, sailor, lonely soul. Goodbye, old friend and lover. Goodbye, may blessings rain on you. Peace. Goodbye. Goodbye, Joe. Go in peace.

6. Now, lay the picture down, hiding the face or let the visualized image fade to nothingness. You have accomplished a lot.

7. Move around, stretch, breathe. Take note of the vacancy where you once held suffering. You are probably tired, for this is exhausting work you've just accomplished. It is wise to honor your fatigue, not try to "ride over" it. It is good to retreat or be with carefully selected companions. Let yourself rest! You've earned it. I predict a surge of energy, yours to do with as you choose, will follow within a few hours or days. Be prepared to feel enthused, exuberant, creative, happy, and welcoming of the rebirth of pleasure!

Since doing your grief work has not induced amnesia, if you are like me, there will be times when thoughts of the person who has died will pour in. For me, it is birth and death days, anniversaries of important events, and holidays. To pretend there isn't a poignant tug is false and unproductive. We must find the line between unhealthy obsessing and wholesome remembrance.

I knew a woman, Helen, whose daughter, Noleen, was killed at seventeen by a drunk driver while the kid was coming home from the library. Helen's grief was deep and proved intractable; her condition became her identity. The most striking evidence was Noleen's bedroom which had been kept as she left it, including dirty socks, unmade bed, and a can of soda on the table. Helen even replaced the bulb that had been left burning so that the reading lamp was perpetually on. She had been visiting the room—which was really a shrine—morning and night (as she did when Noleen was alive) for three years when I met her. Nothing I had to offer made any in-roads, for she was unwilling to move forward in her life. This is an extreme example of a dreadful loss of direction and stagnation of spirit. It is remembrance gone bad.

Just as painful to witness is the total obliteration of evidence that a person had ever lived. When every picture, every memento, every tradition is put away and even a name becomes unspeakable, that becomes persuasive evidence that the necessary grief work has not been done.

Wholesome remembrance finds a balance. After the first months or year of grieving, it seems reasonable to honor the memories with a few pictures, art, or other creations or trophies displayed. These are like a pleasant presence, nostalgic perhaps, but all in all representative of important events and influences.

I have already written of my small observances of Patrick's birth and death days—the red candle, singing "Let It Be," and speaking quietly to his memory about my love for him. I have several gifts from him in my home—a turquoise hippopotamus from the New York Museum of Art and a bit of his pottery—sweet mementos. Let me urge you to find balance, neither worship nor denial, of the memories you share.

My largest memorial to those I have lost to death is this book, because it encompasses the hope and pleasure possible following catastrophic loss.

CHAPTER 9

The Rebirth of Pleasure

I've felt lousy and I've felt great. Believe me, great is better.

—B. A. Elliott

Chaos is to be without form and void. It is more than disorganization, randomness, or confusion. Chaos is *before* any disrupted system and, according to Genesis, it was from this indescribable circumstance that God is said to have created all that exists. Whether or not you accept the version, one certain truth remains: Creation comes from chaos. Things take on order, systems emerge, what never existed comes into being. At its depths, grief is chaotic *and* it is the seedbed of spiritual awakening. I welcome you to this perspective without in any way being presumptuous enough to attempt to direct the nature of your spirituality. I can and have spoken only of my own, not as a model for you to embrace, but as one woman's choice. My hope is you will reestablish or deepen your commitment to a religion, if that is your impulse. If that's not your path, then you must do what all of humankind has done before you: find *your own* way, for it is the only way that is true. Mine has come by immersion in the natural world of an Oregon forest while intimately relating to a river that may someday claim my home and life. I am content to *know* myself as integral with Earth. There are many openings into the spiritual realm. One will be right for you.

Ritual Forty-four: Taking Pleasure Back

This is the time to define yourself in your emerging circumstances. Remember our old friend, ritual 1. On stroke 1, breathe out stagnation, fatigue, resistance, dreariness, despair, or any other feeling that's been haunting you. Be empty of it on stroke 2. For stroke 3, breathe in pure pleasure. Then, finally, be full of pleasure. Repeat until you *know* you are tuned into the possibilities of life.

Bringing Creativity (Back) into Your Life

I think of the creativity that is transmuted from sorrow as the capacity to use experience, talent, and opportunity in ways that bring satisfaction, learning, and vitality. It is a lively process that may produce a work of art, a change in career, or a quantum leap in compassion. In its finest form, it enlightens the spirit and manifests itself as resilience, purpose, and compassion.

We will be changed, but not necessarily reduced, by the death of an intimate or by other sorrows. If we honor our sadness, not pulling away, we may hope to find our talents and viewpoint enhanced when our grief process is resolved. Our innate capacity for understanding others may deepen into empathy that can be a guide and a comfort for those still in the alchemical fire. We will grow in awareness of empowerment as we recognize our progress from chaos to creative living through our own hard work.

Resurgent vitality, desire to be of service, capacity to enjoy, willingness to commit to and receive from others, delight and fun, enjoyment of nature, ability to plan and persevere, and a clear sense of purpose in living—all these are the signs to watch for in charting your progress and the rebirth of pleasure. Each step in refining creative living from the chaos of misery is to be celebrated as it occurs. We are marvelously resilient organisms.

If we choose to break free of our stagnant energy, to cultivate hope rather than live with dreary images, we have passed a critical test for moving on in our lives to greater creativity, fulfillment, and spiritual awareness.

A Good Example

It is a pleasure to share the following material with you. My friend Marjorie, like all of us, lived a life of recurring sorrows but acted as if she could scarcely wait for tomorrow. Marjorie was vigorous to the last moments of her life. My ninety-seven-year-old friend died in a fall while gathering pine needles for her exquisite coiled baskets.

According to her granddaughter, on whose property she lived in a small cottage, "Grandma went for her afternoon walk with Annie Laurie [her Skye terrier]. That was standard after her nap. I realized she hadn't come back about five, when I took over some of her favorite macaroon cookies I'd made, so I went looking.

"She apparently slipped or maybe fainted about a quarter of a mile away, where the big Ponderosa pine is. It had the needles she favored. She was at the bottom of a little rise, on her back. Annie was curled up next to her head. Grandma had a handful of needles in her hand and, believe it or not, she was smiling."

Marjorie was never a client but a dear friend. I have edited the tapes and admit to asking leading questions during the three-year period she spoke with me about her life.

"Sorrow? Troubles? Of course I've had them. Do I look like I sat on a silk cushion all my life? The Buddhists say, 'Life is suffering.' Now, I don't buy that as a be-all and end-all. I'd agree *some* of life is suffering; some of it is boring, some of it is hard work, a lot is loving and helping others out. But the best part you can count on is when you can manage to settle down and make something nice.

"I buried two husbands and one ran away. Each of 'em was a good man in his way. That meant it felt awful when they died or left. I missed 'em. Ed and I got married when I was twenty-four, in 1927. He hurt me bad. After two years he ran off with a blond girl behind the ribbon counter at Woolworth's. Went to Canada and left the baby and me to get by best I could. Those were hard days.

"I couldn't go back to my tap-dancing profession. Not with a baby, and besides, much as I loved it, I'd already done it. Oh, I cried. Didn't want to live, but I had Daisy by then and had to raise her.

"When I was a girl, all the females learned to sew. That's how I made my way. Sewing nice dresses for well-to-do women and costumes for dancers. Oh I loved those costumes—feathers and sequins and lace! I think that helped me get over Ed. Decided he just couldn't help himself. Some men haven't the sense to eat sensible or stop roostering around. Kind of bone headed—sort of pitiful.

"Then, in 1940, I met Tom McGowen. I was thirty-seven years old, which was over the hill and out of sight in those days. He was only thirty-three, so I didn't expect he'd look at me. But he did. He was not all worried about convention or what the neighbors would think. Like me. We got married and it was grand! He was a construction boss. Ran heavy equipment like it was a Swiss watch. He just knew everything about building bridges and what all.

"In 1941 the Japanese bombed Pearl Harbor. Well, he had to go, even though he was married and had a family. In those days, everyone did their part. No slackers. No whiners. Just buckled down and did what had to be done. Tom was killed before he got overseas. In Texas, where he was teaching Seabees about heavy equipment. A tractor backed right over him, broke his back, and he died before I could get there.

"In a way, the war saved me. I had to do my part or else it meant Tom's dying was wasted. I thought like that. After the war, I had a pension and a little ease for the first time. So I learned how to be a fancy chef. Went to school for it, old as I was—mid-forties, by then.

"I loved the smells and the action of the fine restaurant kitchens. Something to do every minute. Would have rather tap danced, but that wasn't practical. I tell you, honey, you're real lucky if you can get a job creating things. You get a sense of accomplishment. And you do some good. Can't beat it. Always look for a job where you get to try new things and use your own judgment. That way, if you make mistakes, they're your mistakes.

"I was alone, after Daisy left, for a long time. Well, not entirely alone. I had company a good deal, but nobody regular in my bed, if that doesn't shock you. But the best part of being alone was being able to do my crafts whenever I wanted. Sometimes, when I first took up tole painting, I would get up at three-thirty or four because I was so excited by an idea. Couldn't sleep, and there was no one I was disturbing.

"You might say I never really accomplished anything that the world will say 'Oh, isn't that wonderful!' about. But I was happy more than I wasn't, which is a pretty good thing to be able to say. The last man I loved, Martin, was a musician. Oh, he made his living before he retired as a bookkeeper, but he was really a musician.

"Martin played the piano. Anything you might want to hear. Ragtime. Chopin. Swing. We loved Gershwin. Martin could sight read music as well as he could read English. Wonderful! He'd play and I'd dance. Got out my tap shoes, even if I was over sixty years old by then. We had hardwood floors, and I would just dance the varnish right off them! We laughed and, honey, that's not all we did!

"I'd say to you that the happiest times of my life were dancing and cooking and painting. Never could make music, even though I could dance any beat anyone could play. Have a tin ear.

"Now I make my pine-needle baskets, and they make people happy after I've had my fun. The fact is, you just have to pull up your socks, find the beat, and keep steppin' out of your misery. Otherwise, then life is just suffering, *and I know that's not how it has to be!*"

Ritual Forty-five: Conscious Choosing

Madelyn, an elementary school teacher, had been on a field trip with second graders when a tire blowing out on an overpass caused an accident. The bus driver was killed and several children seriously hurt. When time had passed, and she was completing her therapy, it was a mark of great progress for her to volunteer to take another class to the zoo on a bus. As she remarked, "I could let the fear of another accident narrow my life, or I could choose to live fully."

This brings to mind Sylvia's succinct poem from her time of trouble.

> *Black dog snarling in the shadows*
> *Call him Despair.*
> *Black dog fetching sticks*
> *Call him Hope.*
> *Which dog will I feed?*

Think of the ways you've narrowed your world during your time of sorrow. This may have manifested as restrictions on relationships, travel, education, curiosity, creative activity, or any other way. Make a list of these restrictions and then a list of actions to break you out of your self-protective rut.

> *Example: I've hidden away, avoiding company. I now resolve to have a meal, go to a show, visit or otherwise meet with old friends once a week for the next six weeks for the potential fun of it. I will make my purpose clear so there is no confusion in my own or my pals' minds.*

Some pleasures are characterized by laughter, a highly desirable thing. For myself, few pleasures equal wordplay—banter—with a quick-witted, well-read person. We're not talking about depth here, but fun. A companion of mine finds pleasure in extraordinarily long walks through the rugged Coast Range of Oregon. A precious person in my life gathers worn wood from beaches and makes gorgeous art from it with nothing more than a jackknife, sandpaper, and stain. Some pleasures are solitary, like reading a truly excellent novel; others convivial, like planning a surprise party. All count, all are important.

Ritual Forty-six: Smiling

- Write a few paragraphs about times you have smiled with pleasure.

- Go through your albums or books and seek out smiling faces. Smile back.

- List movies, books, or activities that have made you happy enough to smile.

- From your work in this ritual, choose which you will actively pursue. Then *do* it!

Pleasurable Service

Teaching and providing are ways of doing service. Service, in this sense, is generosity. You can be generous with time, money, energy, and/or resources. You may share, as I am doing, life experience with those for whom it may be valuable. You can make soup for a shut-in, read to old folks, dig someone's garden, or carry their groceries. This sort of giving is the antithesis of drudging, obligatory, dutiful acts. Pleasurable giving is *not* done because you "should." Pleasurable service is done because it feels good to do: there is satisfaction in it.

And pleasurable giving provides a double reward in refreshing your energy and in renewing your contact with the world.

Ritual Forty-seven: Being of Pleasurable Service

A good place to start is listing the situations, age groups, and activities you enjoy being around. Pick three or four and also list how you can be useful to them without a sense of obligation or hurtful sacrifice.

Example: I like being with children, outdoors, and doing crafts. I could volunteer at the YMCA or school near me for a few lessons, to see how that goes.

At the risk of repeating myself, *now go do it*!

Remember how sweet it was when you caught on to some new idea or principle, maybe picked up a skill? The taste of "ah ha!" is like chilled cantaloupe on a hot day.

Ritual Forty-eight: Learning for Pleasure

Spend some time reflecting on things about which you are curious or skills you'd like to explore. Maybe there is a scholar, artist, composer, or explorer you'd like to know more about. Don't trouble yourself with nonsense that you're too old or it's too hard to work out. Learning can be a supreme pleasure. For our purposes, choose something whose reward is unrelated to job, obligations, or practicality. Learn something because you are following your bliss.

Example: Joseph Campbell, the comparative religions and mythology scholar, fascinates me. I'm going to check out his video and audio tapes from the library and really listen to what he has to say.

Example: I've listened to and watched the Joseph Campbell material as well as reading a good deal. I'm going to organize a study group and see what others think of his ideas.

We don't want to overlook the wonderful potential of the body for pleasure. Every one of the senses offers a pathway. In everyone's life have been moments of sheer physical delight. I once swam nude in a tropical ocean with a porpoise surfing the same waves. And it would be hard to beat Great-grandmother's lemon-meringue pie for gustatory pleasure. Once we learn to associate the body with good feelings, we are always in a pleasure palace.

Ritual Forty-nine: Bodily Delights

In each of the following categories, list at least four or five pleasurable associations from your physical memory:

Touch:

Example: Sliding into a bed with fresh, cool sheets after a good massage.

Taste:

Example: Raspberries!

Smell:

Example: Horses, hot from a ride in the woods.

Hearing:

Example: Bob Marley singing almost anything.

Sight:

Example: Prisms flashing rainbows around my room.

Humor:

Example: Reading Leo Rosten's The Joy of Yiddish.

Your mission, should you choose to accept it (and I believe you have) is to give honest, safe, and appreciate pleasure to each of your senses.

It seems strange that so little is written about the pleasure of spiritual awareness. No matter your spiritual context, it seems evident that Earth and the seasons of nature are integral to all concepts of creation. By this definition, to be in a natural setting or focusing on natural objects is to be in the presence of a spiritual manifestation and such situations are pleasurable.

Ritual Fifty: Getting It All Together

If you possibly can, get outdoors and to a place where your eyes can rest on naturally occurring things. Look for the large—mountains, horizon, stars—and look for the small—dewdrops, spider webs, flowers. Spend time with those things, both animate and inanimate. Breathe and use all the tools of aware participation you've learned in our time together.

If you cannot get physically to such a place, there are other possibilities. One, of course, is your mind, your imagination. Another is holding an amulet such as a shell or antler. Geodes are nice for this.

To use your senses in harmony with mind, emotions, and spirit is to experience pleasure. The tools exist to further your awareness and provide ways to practice. Having discovered your capacity for sorrow, you now know that you have equal potential for pleasure. You have practiced some skills in the rituals of this book, all can be expanded and repeated. Having the tools, vision, and motivation, you can look forward to life, assured you are well-equipped to live pleasurably.

Long ago, trying to crystallize my thinking-feeling-physical philosophy, I wrote the following piece. Perhaps it will sum up and suggest some useful principles. Even though we've finished the rituals for this book, I can't resist suggesting you write your own credo to bring this process to a wholesome finish.

Credo for Seasons of Life

There is an incomprehensible Great Mystery beyond all categories of thought, even those of being and non-being.
The Great Mystery is outside of time, space, and duality.
Soul is of the Great Mystery, therefore external.
Soul exists whether incarnate or not.
Soul loss is the most serious condition.

Soul life must be cultivated.
Spirit is an aspect of Soul.
Spirit animates and informs all parts of Creation.
Self is the unitary wholeness of body, mind, emotion, and spirit.
Body and mind are lovers.
Emotion is their child.
Our Seasons of Life are lived upon the Great Spiral.
The Great Spiral endlessly returns to the Great Mystery.
Change is constant.
Transformation is inevitable.
We live in the duality of time and space.
Growth and entropy are equally potential.
To have consciousness is to have choice.
All have suffered.
Anguish and ecstasy are equally potential.
Myth, ceremony, Sacred Space, and Dedicated Time are natural expressions of numinous truth.
Predators exist.
Allies exist.
Fulfillment exists.
Reconciliation with natural life is possible.
Action is necessary.
Stamina is required.
Courage is indispensable.
Quiet is essential.
Hope is breath.
Happiness is vital.
Creativity opens to the numinous.
Love is primary.
Death is the scaffold for the Web of Life.
Life is to be lived. Now.

Peace and pleasure to you.

References

Achterberg, Jeanne. 1985. *Imagery in Healing: Shamanisim and Modern Medicine*. New York: Random House.

Benson, Herbert. 1975. *The Relaxation Response*. New York: Morrow.

Borysenko, Joan, and Larry Rothstein. 1988. *Minding the Body, Mending the Mind*. New York: Bantam.

Eden, Donna. 1999. *Energy Medicine*. New York: Tarcher.

Gawain, Shakti. 1982. *Creative Visualization*. New York: Bantam.

Goldstein, Joseph, and Jack Kornfield. 1987. *Seeking the Heart of Wisdom: The Path of Insight Meditation*. Boston: Shambhala.

LeShan, Lawrence. 1984. *How to Meditate: A Guide to Self-Discovery*. New York: Bantam.

O'Donohue, John. 1996. *Anam Cara: Wisdom from the Celtic World*. Boulder: Sounds True.

Progoff, Ira. 1975. At a Journal Workshop: *The Basic Text and Guide for Using the Intensive Journal Process*. New York: Dialogue House Library.

Thich Nhat Hahn. 1976. *The Miracle of Mindfulness: A Manual on Meditation*. Boston: Beacon.

photo by Robert Hunt

Peg Elliott Mayo, LCSW, is a psychotherapist with forty years' experience. She worked in a wide array of institutional jobs early in her career and has been in private practice for thirty years. Her work makes active use of principles from Gestalt Therapy and modern Jungian practices, within a context of respect for the body and the fostering of individual spiritual exploration.

Peg lives in the forest in Oregon's Coast Range with a good man, two remarkable dogs, and too many cats. She is a basketry and clay artist whose works have been widely displayed in fine galleries. She has an intimate relationship with a beautiful river.

Some Other New Harbinger Self-Help Titles

Juicy Tomatoes, $13.95
Help for Hairpullers, $13.95
The Anxiety & Phobia Workbook, Third Edition, $19.95
Thinking Pregnant, $13.95
Rosacea, $13.95
Shy Bladder Syndrome, $13.95
The Adoption Reunion Survival Guide, $13.95
The Queer Parent's Primer, $14.95
Children of the Self-Absorbed, $14.95
Beyond Anxiety & Phobia, $19.95
The Money Mystique, $13.95
Toxic Coworkers, $13.95
The Conscious Bride, $12.95
The Family Recovery Guide, $15.95
The Assertiveness Workbook, $14.95
Write Your Own Prescription for Stress, $13.95
The Shyness and Social Anxiety Workbook, $15.95
The Anger Control Workbook, $17.95
Family Guide to Emotional Wellness, $24.95
Undefended Love, $13.95
The Great Big Book of Hope, $15.95
Don't Leave it to Chance, $13.95
Emotional Claustrophobia, $12.95
The Relaxation & Stress Reduction Workbook, Fifth Edition, $19.95
The Loneliness Workbook, $14.95
Thriving with Your Autoimmune Disorder, $16.95
Illness and the Art of Creative Self-Expression, $13.95
The Interstitial Cystitis Survival Guide, $14.95
Outbreak Alert, $15.95
Don't Let Your Mind Stunt Your Growth, $10.95
Energy Tapping, $14.95
Under Her Wing, $13.95
Self-Esteem, Third Edition, $15.95
Women's Sexualitites, $15.95
Knee Pain, $14.95
Helping Your Anxious Child, $12.95
Breaking the Bonds of Irritable Bowel Syndrome, $14.95
Multiple Chemical Sensitivity: A Survival Guide, $16.95
Dancing Naked, $14.95
Why Are We Still Fighting, $15.95
From Sabotage to Success, $14.95
Parkinson's Disease and the Art of Moving, $15.95
A Survivor's Guide to Breast Cancer, $13.95
Men, Women, and Prostate Cancer, $15.95
Make Every Session Count: Getting the Most Out of Your Brief Therapy, $10.95
Virtual Addiction, $12.95
After the Breakup, $13.95
Why Can't I Be the Parent I Want to Be?, $12.95
The Secret Message of Shame, $13.95
The OCD Workbook, $18.95
Tapping Your Inner Strength, $13.95
Binge No More, $14.95
When to Forgive, $12.95
Practical Dreaming, $12.95
Healthy Baby, Toxic World, $15.95
Making Hope Happen, $14.95
I'll Take Care of You, $12.95
Survivor Guilt, $14.95
Children Changed by Trauma, $13.95
Understanding Your Child's Sexual Behavior, $12.95
The Self-Esteem Companion, $10.95
The Gay and Lesbian Self-Esteem Book, $13.95
Making the Big Move, $13.95
How to Survive and Thrive in an Empty Nest, $13.95
Living Well with a Hidden Disability, $15.95
Overcoming Repetitive Motion Injuries the Rossiter Way, $15.95
What to Tell the Kids About Your Divorce, $13.95
The Divorce Book, Second Edition, $15.95
Claiming Your Creative Self: True Stories from the Everyday Lives of Women, $15.95
Taking Control of TMJ, $13.95
What You Need to Know About Alzheimer's, $15.95
Winning Against Relapse: A Workbook of Action Plans for Recurring Health and Emotional Problems, $14.95

Call **toll free, 1-800-748-6273**, or log on to our online bookstore at **www.newharbinger.com** to order. Have your Visa or Mastercard number ready. Or send a check for the titles you want to New Harbinger Publications, Inc., 5674 Shattuck Ave., Oakland, CA 94609. Include $4.50 for the first book and 75¢ for each additional book, to cover shipping and handling. (California residents please include appropriate sales tax.) Allow two to five weeks for delivery.

Prices subject to change without notice.